SO FAR

SELECTED POEMS
1960–2004

Jonty Driver

SNAILPRESS/JOHN CATT EDUCATIONAL LTD

Published by
SNAILPRESS, 30 Firfield Road, Plumstead, 7800, South Africa and
JOHN CATT EDUCATIONAL LIMITED, Great Glemham, Saxmundham,
Suffolk, IP17 2DH, United Kingdom
Email SA: *snail@pulsar.co.za* or UK: *enquiries@johncatt.co.uk*

ISBN 1-904724-27-2
First published 2005
© C J Driver 2005

Cover photograph by Annari van der Merwe
Author's photograph by Ellen Elmendorp
Design and typesetting by User Friendly, Cape Town, South Africa
Printed and bound by Mills Litho, Cape Town, South Africa

CONTENTS

Transvaal afternoon

The tall white house stands silently
In the heat of a Transvaal afternoon,
Between the mountains and the water,
Halfway between the sun and the trees.
Insects move slowly across the heat.
    There is danger of fire
In the pine-trees around my home:
You can see the farm-men look up,
Every now and again, watching for smoke;
The women keep their heads down.
All you hear is earth moving, cars
Across the river on the road
Through the plantations, and the drone
Of heat-flies.
    Up at my home
It would be cooler, as the air moves
Where the land lifts. But here,
Even your hands sweat. The sun
Slaps down across the lowveld.
      Nothing
Has much meaning here, where the sun
Strikes. The red dust is still, tick-birds
Sit in a tree above the water, men
And women working do not talk,
Even curse the heat. The sun gropes
At your body and at the lowveld.
      But later,
When I go home, the lowveld will close
Around me, and the wind will move
Suddenly through the house.

With a rifle

The leaves of your green age rattle
On the windows: it's the rifle, iron
And the burnt wood are borders
Of my lowveld country, where the lion

And impala, all die against fences.
– Where the heart lies, lies our fear –
The prints harden as the sun hardens:
What I listen for, I cannot hear,

Cannot, for my life, know anything
Against this, the blood and the steel,
Death in the long grass, where the thorn
Tears you, and snake strikes the heel.

The reeds whip blood to your skin
As the lowveld lifts itself about you,
Like an animal, waking, suddenly;
Has a movement like the death of you,

Like the water, watching, and the feel
Of leaves' veins in your fingers, things
That have history, just like love
And just like hate. The sand clings

To your feet, and holds you hard
Against the lowveld. The rivers wait
For a false movement, a stone sliding
And breath caught against the mouth
Of your fear. Where the rifle's side

Is cold against your fingers, a part
Of your memory moves behind you,
And you turn quickly, and watch:
– Where the heart lies, lies our fear –
But nothing moves except the wind.

Johannesburg

The mine-heads reach to the sky,
Or the sky is falling.
    We mourn for our country.

The river that I drink is dry,
My name is silence, my chief is anger,
And I work for hatred, all day long.
    We mourn for our country.

Out of the hot sun's cave
We crawl to our caves,
Out of the bush-grass burning
We burn in our fires.
    We mourn for our country.

The bricks of the city cry out,
Louder than the people.
    We mourn for our country.

My face giggles in a blackened mirror,
My hands clock at the scars.
    We mourn for our country.

The blind man, time, makes spittle with his coin.
Metals on his tongue
Grope like mine-dust into his lungs.
    We mourn for our country.

Whistle the wild bird, the feather.
    We mourn for our country.

Elegy for my contemporaries

Bones on a telegraph-pole
Dance their epitaph
To those born rich and healthy,

Young men, clean-limbed, clear-eyed,
Those who wore the clothes
Of dying children.

They were not without love
Or beauty; their hands were tied
To the wheels of brilliance

And they whirled like gunfire
In the night. I name them
Among my friends, my people,

Those who married well, who loved
Their children, who gave
What their pockets allowed.

They shall die in their doorways
And in the streets, thrombosis
And murder pay their debts –

You cannot count them now, the lines
Of soldiers who drank deeply
From the jewelled cup of safety.

A ballad of hunters

My great-grandfather hunted elephants,
Shot four hundred in a year,
Till one day his death turned round
And sniggered in his ear.

> *The theme's the same, the method changes –*
> *Time has planned the ending,*
> *Has turned the hunter to the hunted*
> *And bred the next from nothing.*

My great-great-uncle farmed alone,
Made next to nothing from his land,
Till at last the cancer took him,
Eating from his living hand.

> *The theme's the same, the method changes –*
> *Time has planned the ending,*
> *Has turned the farmer to the harvest*
> *And bred the next from nothing.*

Cousins and cousins in their dozens
Were killed in their mission churches
By the tribes whose heads they broke
To teach them the Christian virtues.

> *The theme's the same, the method changes –*
> *Time has planned the ending,*
> *Has turned the clergy to the converts*
> *And bred the next from nothing.*

My father's father died in northern France,
Shooting Germans for his British past –
Left his wife a private's pension
And children to make it last.

The theme's the same, the method changes –
Time has planned the ending,
Has turned the sniper to the target
And bred the next from nothing.

Both my uncles fought the war,
Like lovers died a year apart –
Left some letters and a flag or two
And silence to be their art.

The theme's the same, the method changes –
Time has planned the ending,
Has turned the fighters to the dying
And bred the next from nothing.

Now I'm my subject, a sort of hunter
Stalking the blood of my family –
But hunted too by time's revenge
For all they made of my history.

To Jann, in her absence

If she asks why the sun
Knocks so loudly at the window,
Tell her nothing but a shadow
Has so much permanence
As love, that has nothing
But doubt to feed on.

If she asks why her love
Speaks so quietly of a closed house
In the city, a window
Where the light cannot come in,
Tell her no one but traitors
Walk as quietly as love.

These are images I have made
From my loneliness, have carved
From the stone of my country,
Have woven like blankets
For my sleep. These images
Sing as quietly as love.

A poem for Jann

I

It is always dark when you leave me,
The light's gone out behind your door,
And I walk home alone and longingly.

Not so much as love we lovers long for,
But a sort of knowledge, something
To break the anarchy of reason, a law

Of the trees that crowd around me and cling
Like shadows to my heels. The hours
Bark like dogs. It is this or nothing.

II

Right at the bottom of the hill's my home,
Down an old street without any light,
With one tree for a garden. There's my home

Where shadows whisper and the long night
Closes me round with my head-
Long desires. So many shadows blur my sight.

Like children our playground's all in the head,
Is all a fiction and uncertainty,
Leaving what we most believe in all unsaid.

In the end we must go back to simplicity,
Night and love in the quiet houses,
And the always dark when you leave me.

A love song

Brittle as glass, my woman;
If I touch her she will break.
So do not come too close –
This is a most private place.

Under her left breast, on her palm,
I found my private marks –
She has made hers in my face,
Privately in that public place.

The hurt forms part of her beauty,
The scars breathe beauty themselves;
Nowadays I own nothing of her
But a brittle time of her flesh.

But will she ever let me free?
I am held by the glass of self
To her secret gaze of hurt
And her lovely privacy of flesh.

O do not come too close –
This is a most private place;
It's the traitor glass I cry for
That sees her in my face.

In solitary confinement, Sea Point police cells

In the early morning
  when the light and the sea smell come stumbling in
    (salt, sea, sun, and the green
       imagined breakers)

I greet the shadows
  with the names of my brothers and sister
    and watch them coil and yawn
       on morning's grey wall.

I breed a new sense
  to learn the secrets known to the sea
    how our drowning flesh dissolves
       until yellow the bones

Go rolling, rolling
  into generation of sand, shell and sandstone
    and leave only the rise and the fall of the seas'
       far Atlantic roll.

A public man confesses his private longings

Bald mother moon and your children,
Bless my country, bless my continent,
Bless the white cattle in the lands
Where the tribes gather
And the green sea-branches
That wave over us.

Bless her silence, bless her loveliness,
Bless the hair that curls like a hand
Over her nakedness.

Bless my image
Of the witching girl, a stone's throw from the church,
Dying so quietly that no one could hear
And the hero running, though her answer told him
That all the waters were closed round her head.

Shine like gold on the great snake's back
That bred us and bears our children
In the tall mountain we call home,
In whose quiet I shall be found,
Visionary, with the light around me,
And each existence moving light,
And each light stillness.

Birthdays

Aged twenty-six
I am afraid to die,
That last night's dream
Of an old, fat-faced man
Trapped in a war of sweat
Might take my face from me.

Aged twenty-five
I caught a disease
Of each alone in a cage,
Who in goes striding
And out comes crawling
To daily dying flesh.

Aged twenty-four
I saw how hunger
Shoved its thin fingers
Into each skin and eye
Till abstractions lived
In define of bone.

Aged twenty-three
I spoke out bravely,
Named the people's needs –
Declared my private war,
Great abstractions made
Of love and death and pain.

These celebrations of age
Have jumped each fact
With new lust, new flesh –
Till I trouble my bones
With a love each year
And each love a last.

But I am devised
Only a means to die;
What is now, what was,
Must share my cage
With that fat-faced man
Who comes, my age himself.

Poem about exile

for Harry Cohen

All this is guesswork, an order based on small fact
And word-lust. It will not break one bone of exile.

It is an easy way to disguise the flesh of despair
As a hesitation in the voice, a small diffidence,
When it would cry out, 'God save us, save us' –
For my gods are only words dressed up like poems.

Various marks stumble darkly on a white page.
They go, my brave explorers, across their continents
Into the green, green summer.
                              There they shall rest.
Proudly my gods blow and puff their poor feathers.

Poem for a higher degree

Osney Island, Oxford

These days my home is
    out of the mountains,
an island, a street, a house
        on the edge
    of water green or brown
        as studies take us –

confused by light, by cold,
    by easy winds, those
by flood un-iced. The weir roars;
        the lock-gates
    are never undone. The ice states:
        easy it does.

All day the tanker loads
    its roar of oil
into next door's storage.
        All night I leave
    my curtains open, catch
        the water-light

against white walls and ceiling,
    blue sheets and blankets,
my safety house. All day I am drawn
        to the weir;
    all night I sleep
        in the tanker's void.

Fragment

A sudden sea wind, something of winter,
    Chasing the sand –
    (A girl's way of moving,
Forgotten across an absence of years)
    You said something
    I could not hear;
What the hard rain of winter seasons
Has swept to bare root and white rock.

Patrick Duncan in hospital

The friends around his bed
Do not speak of the dead
Wasted country.
He turns to see
Past their heads how the Londoned air
Daubs and scrapes his exile there.

It makes no difference now.
Blood eats blood, but how
We do not know.
Justice too is slow.
There are such things done by men to men
We can hardly bear to hear them again.

High above London he lies,
Never doubtful now. His eyes
Do not pretend
Disease will end –
Where sun has flaked and knived colonial hills,
Death is a drought of blood that only kills.

And yet, every single last
Loss must burst from its past –
Like dying. So,
He died; and so
Remember Patrick Duncan, who to the end
Faced the faceless dark as a friend.

To the dark, singing

i.m. John Harris, executed in 1965 for sabotage and murder,
who went to his death singing, 'We shall overcome'.

This man's no hero; mad, perhaps,
Killed an old woman and burned
A child's face to a white skull
So he might make a god out of pain
To free his country from the praise
Of a golden beast. But we are fools
Who dose our disease with hate,
    Though we sing when we die.

No praise then; and no prayer either –
For we are past the praying stage.
All prayers shout out too loudly
When one man goes alone to die
In a short falling, a short way
Through his little dark to the dark,
    Though he sings when he dies.

Each of us makes a separate peace
With the dark; he made his cruelly
Both ways, that his beast of fire
Might gobble the other golden beast
And the sweet smell of flesh
Burning, burning, might crowd the gate
Where his country waits, unspeaking,
    Though it sang when he died.

I can see no beauty in this
Except that a man should sing
To his dark
Till the rope breaks his voice –

The flames burn white in his skull,
And no one death repeats another,
    Though he sang when he died.

The return of terror

Variations on a theme

I

Footsteps outside on the ice of the driveway;
Keep still in my chair (the shadows in movement)
Hoping that no one will come. In an absence
Of light and a sighing of wind, nothing comes in;
Nothing remembers a name and approaches. But I say,
Light on the snow from the window deceived me,
Light of the snow corrupting the glass. So undone
The deception is done. At that he comes in.

II

Now terror returns, like a blind child calling –
Blind eyes moving, cavernous eyes of howls
And whispers, and scars of my fatherly fingers
Defacing his cheeks. So I turn in my chair
To my son at the window, or son at the door,
Calling *Come on and come in*; nothing returns
And I wait in my chair for the handle to turn
And an absence of love and a stranger come in.

III

Terror returns; and down is not fall or a falling,
Only a scar. *You were dreaming*, says my wife
As she wakes me; *you called out a name.*
Whose was that name? Keep back firmly turned
In the bed, saying *Terror returned.* If I dream
Of a face or a voice, or cry out that name,
It is only an image for that which I waking
Dare not remember. Dream between dream and descent.

IV

I dream what follows myself. What is past
Is still in my dream of the past, and what is –
The coming about, the coming apart – is the dead
In a circle of eyes. If they saw, I could bear it
But I join in the circle and stare blindly out:
And terror returns. Pray for the dead newly dead
And the dead long past, and the footsteps
Of nothing that slide on the ice of the driveway.

In a darkened late Victorian room

As man I know
The laws
Like *Light will equal peace*
Or sometimes *Light will cease;*
As beast I break them, or as god.

So too the dancers,
Those whose bodies leap and souls
Are lighter than the light-blown leaves
Of early winter.

In this darkened late Victorian room
I crouch
And wait for coming light
To flap in through the trees
With eyes like souls, and wings, and claws –

(How often now my image is a room
From which I watch the brighter light outside
Or darker dark
Hover there and glide
Above my perfectly perfected inside light.)

And nothing comes:
The winds can't shake the trees;
Those dancers, on their knees,
Whose static dancing at the air
They imitate, are frozen now.
A god
Comes near; yet will they stir?
They wait. *A beast comes,*
Their branches cry.
But it is only dark.
Not I!
As beast I crouch, or scream, a minor god.

So in this darkened late Victorian room
I wait;
Beyond the light of one small lamp
The darkness steadily grows darker still.
And then the night.
And nothing comes.

Yet still I cannot move.
For all the dancers' guidance,
Still I cannot move.

There is a new law now:
Like danger looms the light.

What the stones said to Michael Rostrow

Postscript to 'False Impossible Shore' in Penguin *Modern Stories 8*

I

Believe us. We are the ones who wait.
We do not think. We know a little truth.
We threaten only what we understand.

II

When love speaks to us, we do not stir –
What blood falls on us, the rain will wash
Away. We grow less, but only very slowly.

III

And when we break, the eventual earth
Will make us whole again. The years
Are our compatriots, rain and quicksand.

IV

We only seem immobile. In the mind of God
We dance. You see, we are his children.
You have seen our purple shadows walking.

V

Us you must not touch too surely. Our voices
Learn the ways of men, and when we speak
Men keep silence. Believe us when you hear our voices.

For the anonymous dead

Nowhere that we cannot find them now,
The lately dead, the soon forgotten –

Those who fell because the earth tilted,
The trampled dead, the dead from their time,

Who list no dates but the big years,
Who raise no funds for public monuments.

The wind around the house-eaves mourns
For dead forests under the marshes,

The wind in the pine-trees too remembers
The death of flame. Everything passes ...

There is no sense in repeating the fact.
These died privately for no praise or gain,

Bled like heroes, starved like great men,
Were kindly led into camps or ovens,

Crashed when the driver of the other car
Sneezed, or God for that matter blinked,

Were bombed without hate from a great height,
Or buried alive in the ash. We remember

No names at all; they hardly matter at all,
Not to the way we live, not to our breathing.

The plural of no one doesn't exist,
Only the half-burned face of a newsprint child.

One way of looking

for Ann

There's one way of looking that sees
An intricate weave of emotion
In every move of the leaves –
You can hardly tell them apart,
The death of desire, the urge of the seed.

I have moved out of sunlight – the woods
Are my intricate home, though my eyes
Were made for a distance, not my hands
For this detail of delicate bones.

There are places to lie in the warmth
Of these woods; but the dark always dark
Makes room for my blindness – you learn this
By touching, then sleep through the day.

Sometimes she wakes and she calls me.
I go by the sound, though my hands
Are always before me. She's gone by that time.
I am learning the different names of the trees
And, when I learn light, I shall see her.

Dark wood with occasional light and wind

The more that it shines, the more fails
*   The occasional light; the more fails*
*   The less we can bear not to look ...*

I

Black day, or say blank, since I lack
    More perfectly needing perfection;
    Or say that I'm useless at small-talk.

That is not meant in the doing of things;
    It is all in the words, cerebration
    Of certainty, certainty doubted,

The devils of ache, of regret, of lament:
    Things turned to words in the house
    And sighed for a place with the dead.

II

So I escaped, drove to my private dark wood
    (Where only myself would be racked
    With my lack of the right slight words),

Walked in the trees. But the wind-voices sighed
    And the devils rampaged in the leaves,
    Throwing the dust of the light in my eyes ...

III

Once silence fell in a wood; first it became
    Like a leaf, then like a branch, later
    A tree (my own roof-tree my scaffold)

And the wind made it talk, and it talked
    Like the souls of the dead, till I thought
    I too was a dead man in the wild dark wood.

Blood from the breaking of leaves; the wind
 Eating the flesh of my hands, my eyes
 Greying like stone, and my voice

Like wind in the pine, in the oak, in the beech,
 In the crevice of the fallen elm.
 Under the elm was the stone.

Under the stone the most unspeakable quiet
 Was the chatter
 Of crumbling earth ...

IV

Back to my home with the house-guests talking.
 I have no desire to be
 Like a stone.

I will willingly sacrifice light; I will join
 In every trivial talking of words.
 I resign from my grave in the woods.

The more that it shines, the more fails
 The occasional light; the more fails,
 The less we can bear not to look ...

To a child coming in winter

So far, my fourth winter
Has not landed.
        I see him circle the clouds
Like a wide-winged hawk,
But he has not landed.

The edge of his flight
Cuts the leaves down.
        My wife walks cautious as a cat;
She comes safely down the steps
On her long thin legs.

I ask for my child
To be born with the snow.
        Three English winters alone,
I want this one crowded.
He's not ready, she says.

Still, the sweep of his growth
Curves like the flight of a hawk.
        I can see wings fluttering in her
Almost like hands;
The clouds look almost like snow.

The end-ground

Any man, walking a (let's say) Cornish beach,
Might stop, for no apparent sign,
And lift a stone, one particular white
And half-warm stone, and lift it up
And might then say aloud
(As if to prove his touch) 'A stone'.

And what would the stone say?
A single word, like 'harsh' or 'cold',
Or even 'sleep'? The stone says
Nothing that he hears. He could, but daren't, break
Upon another harder stone this lack
Of air, this atomed multiplicity;

And so he'd put it down again
In that same hollowed earth it made
Some days (or years) ago when tide
Had rolled it from a sea-bed home
Of greens and blues and water-notes
Of sea on shells on sounding stones.

And, yards away, he'd turn to listen
Whether now the stone would make
Some small, some sea-returning sound,
Perhaps a word like 'man', or 'god';
But stone has much the voice that air has,
The same that now succeeds
– With no apparent sign – this other voice …

What Heyst said

I have come, the darkness says; to which the sea replies
In whispers which will hardly reach the burning house
Upon the island, *Remember me and be afraid.*

This dark delights me; it staggers like a child
Uncertain of the ground below him, and then speaks,
Child pretending, *I will not sleep again, no, not ever.*

The sea has no need to threaten that. *I am not afraid,*
Says my son, half-asleep, but will not let me go.
The house is drifting out to sleep

As if the island too were drifting out to sea,
Massed and steady, and alive again,
Moving with the air against the swing of earth.

To make myself feel safe, I say aloud:
My son is sleeping now; my wife is reading
In her bed, and I am writing this …

Breathing slow, I trust myself upon the air.
Welcome, says the sea. Men in clean white robes
Are gathered on the headland, waving branches …

Rule my kingdom, drowning sailor, says the sea.
O save me, save, calls the sailor
For I shall sleep too cold on these hard shores.

The men are gathered now upon the shore,
The rocks are speaking, blood is gathered up
Like crops of seaweed. Light is gathered on the waves …

My son has woken; *afraid*, he cries, *afraid*.
Afraid I comfort him. How strange my sleep must seem
To those who teach me love; how slow the learning

Not to be afraid – and yet the sea returns
And love is taken up into the air. *Not dark, my son,*
That you must fear, but too much light ...

As policemen choose the brightest cleanest rooms
To ask their questions in, so worse diseases grow
Than we have dreamt of, underneath a microscope ...

And yet I say, I search for light; and so the sea
Remembers me, gravely makes my home. *Unknown foreign sailor,*
Note the watchers on the headland, begin a prayer ...

Witness this, my wife, my sleeping son. *That man*
Is lost who learns too late to love. Remember me
Asleep and walking in my private loveless light.

Small poem for a small boy

Behind the town
The fields with broken hedges lie
Like ragged handkerchiefs
Laid out to dry.

Lincolnshire fenland

If you take it largely, this land
Has no distinction, though looking close
You see the speckling of the grass by wind,
The waterlights of leaves, an old grey horse
Cropping in a ditch. But the long way
From here to that horizon gives the eye
Sky-room. It is often drawn away and up;
When light on the ploughed field shifts, you look
Up at the clouds to verify the shapes
Of all their reaches ...
                              The things you see
Explain themselves: the clouds, the leaves, the ditch.
Horizon, wind and light do not – none is seen
Except in change or absence. Yet this light
And that horizon hold their objects, make
Borders to the state of being here, and now –
A scape of verbs, not nouns, since it needs
Conjugation. This is lightscape for the restless,
For refugees and exiles. This is landscape
For settlers, the socially immobile, private
People who watch small beasts in hedgerows,
The speckling grass, the leaves spilling light,
And not the random emphases of wind on clouds.

Domestic scene, with monsters

Through the kitchen window, my wife
Hanging wet sheets on an awkward line;

The Third slightly distorting a piano;
Whitsun trippers running down the street;

The breakfast still untidy on the table;
The sunlight dusty on the window pane ...

What one is after is a holding of things:
The sense of people joined in crowded houses;

Thoroughly modern desire, despite the wind
Which flaps the sheets up and outwards now.

One perceives so much of what one wants to,
Muddling expectation with the now-to-come,

Yet still imagines such hopeless monsters
In other places, with human senses searching

Still for children, wives, and good mornings,
In a small town of very ordinary people.

There were no such places, say the monsters,
Mooning sadly through inter-galactic spaces.

Early morning, from a train, near Johannesburg

*'the cyanide process ... consists in steeping the finely crushed ore in
a solution of sodium cyanide in the presence of air, when the gold
dissolves as the auro-cyanide complex ion ... From the sodium auro-
cyanide solution the gold is precipitated by the addition of zinc.'*

It is more than a life in my past
That I woke in the dawn on the train
And thought that what woke me was only
The white cyanide of the mine-dumps
That hump from the base of Johannesburg:
To get gold add a poisonous salt
And air for its poisonous breathing.

Not dust in my lungs that awoke me –
Incipient poison – but halo of dust
Round the sun. In the white, the watery light
Was refracted, then wavered and broke
Into gold. A man on the opposite bunk
Coughed and spat from the window; 'the dust
From those damnable things,' he complained.

Yet mine-dumps have uses: that they make
Such a place for the dawn's careful
Investment of sun is a use, that they make
One amazed at the gold that fell down.
The dawn is made out of gold in that air,
And mine-dumps themselves could be gold
As they sepulchre smoky Johannesburg.

It was hard to imagine it then
As wicked Johannesburg, 'city of thieves',
A Gomorrah engilded, an updated Chicago,
The stink of the Sixties, and Seventies too
(And the devil knows what of the Eighties:
Say Berlin as it fell, or say Sparta,
Or St Petersburg burning and burning ...)

Yet all I remember now is that sun:
How it looked like the singular eye
Of wicked, exciting Johannesburg,
While I watched from the train in a past
That is poisoned and holy, a dream
Of the dead awaiting their dead, and the gold
Coming down through the air, like gold.

On Bloemfontein

For ten years I've been avoiding the thought
Of you under the ground, of what earth does
To a coffin, and worse to what is inside;
I wouldn't go to see you in your coffin,
Not to see you dead, because I didn't
Want to believe it. And I made them wait
Before they threw the earth and stones on
So not to hear the sound, although the sound
Remains a metaphor of considerable falling.
And now I remember, watching my own
Decay, my face assume your lines, the hair
Recede, the stomach advance, and friends who say
I grow more like you every day,
I here in England, and you under the ground,
In Bloemfontein (flower-fountain in Dutch,
And a bad city, as bad as most, but worse
In Dutch) and I can't see flowers at all,
Only the fall of your ten years' death.

Home and exile

I read outside, in the sun.
They are rioting in my old country.

Near me, four English students
Are playing a game of dice.

The open windows of the university
Are graced with lawns and water.

The fountain flares like a mane
When the wind eludes the buildings.

The tribe I used to belong to
Rides through a dying country.

In the fragmented light of the fountain
The dice fall like stones at their feet.

I am English, and slightly northern.
I said, my friend, that I live here now.

York, 1976

Letter to Breyten Breytenbach from Hong Kong

Another holiday.
              The kids away,
My wife, the dogs; I here, alone at home,
Working, as always, with words, while they play
Sporadic games on a beach, and miss me
To catch the high ones, or fetch the picnic
From the car park.
                  Musing on you, I write
With my head still buried in Africa,
Which I abandoned, when I was younger,
Before it abandoned me, or stranded
Someone a little like me then,
For the years I did not care to barter
For my own or someone else's freedom.

Now in front of my window a blank wall
And coils of wire – conditional enterprise
To keep the felons out, to keep me in,
In a great city on the edge of China;
And I remember you in gaol, whom no one
Trusts any more, not entirely.
                      Van Wyk,
Named 'Spyker', has obviously learned by now
How to fish for poets, both thin and tall –
You catch them with words, a little bit bent
And baited with action. They are too trusting
For words. You pull the buggers in like eels.
They pant under the lights.
                 In Pollsmoor Prison
You joke with the warders – a traitor, true,
But still their kind, the *volk*. The prison governor,
Whose mind is almost his own, commissions
(Not too abstract!) paintings. Poems are harder;
You can't be always sure that what they say
They really mean: they might be in a code
Or tell your readers what is best concealed.

It must be hard to try to represent
A revolution when you want to be
A revelation. Out of words we make
Sporadic fictions, now and sometimes then.

Since I am hardly what I seem to be
What seems to me may not be you at all –
For self-concealing me, read you, romantic:
Your France, my England; your Pollsmoor Prison,
My Asian exile. Yet we must be shared …
The world feasts on writers, especially
When they're wrong. You cannot mean those lies.
And yet you meant them, just as I meant mine.

Oh, Breyten Breytenbach, we take our gaols
On our backs like pilgrims, and Giant Despair
Inhabits cities anywhere airlines
Care to dump us and our lame histories.
The choices that we make are not so sure
As policemen think, and what we make ourselves
Flickers like gunfire over the borders.
Traitors are traitors, even our own kind;
We gave away our future long ago.

Quintet

About time too

At four in the morning, I wake
To look at the strange lights
In the foreign harbour.

Across the dark and silver water
The exiled ghosts go home
To their distorted distance.

Tensions of light
String from anchored boats
To anchored buildings,
And something like contentment here I note
To see so little so late.

I have no past, no people;
I belong nowhere now –
Here in the water-margins
Of China
And history.

Not quite

Home at nine, after a long day
At desk, interviews and meetings
With that ache more of eyes than head
Like a slow progress up stairways
With small prospect of arrival.
    Not quite, I said, not quite.

Meaning not very much, I guess,
Being polite, or meaning more
But not the end, not absolute
As if by saying that I tried
To turn aside what might be worse.
    Not quite, I said, not quite.

Being busy and middle-aged,
I have the usual fantasies
Of return and recognition:
There are times when I even seem
Something like my own father was.
    Not quite, I said, not quite.

Walking in town with my tall son
We were stopped by a red-faced tourist:
How very much alike you seem,
Your father's son, your son like you.
I stammered back, embarrassedly:
    Not quite, I said, not quite.

How little now I have to say
About the things concerned me once.
Sons matter more than politics;
It is the milkman knocks at dawn;
My country recedes to headlines –
    Not quite, I said, not quite.

Somewhere else

One grows used to it in the end, I guess,
The condition of exile. One talks of one as one
And writes one's love songs to the Emperor
Who sent one packing to a far-off town
In a province of harsh barbarians.
We know all about exiles in China
Says my scholarly friend in the grey silk:
A poet's home is always somewhere else –
No one ever sees again the cloud-cloth
Draping the mountains, the white waters foam
Among the pine-trees, the bright-speared aloes;
These are images of childhood, not place –
We see ourselves in time.
                              Shall I never,
Never again see the lowveld? Never.
Shall I never hear the hadedahs call
In the dusk across Grahamstown, nor smell
The pepper-corns in the rectory sand-pit?
One grows used to it in the end, I guess –
And one does one's best not to remember;
One does one's best to think. One learns to smile
At strangers who stare at one in the street,
At the clack-clack-clack of their dialect.
It is the dust which makes my face look grey,
And the north monsoon which reddens my eyes.
The Emperor was, as I said, quite crazy,
And the fire leaping across the tree-tops
Explodes like gunfire in the black townships.

Now and then

The face on the torn page
Under the headline,
The torn face on the page –

That it should come to this
At midnight on a Sunday,
On the edge of China

More than half a lifetime
Swept out like dust
From a corner of my mind

And what seems tragic is not
Heroes in a death cell
But a child on a road-side

An angry farmer in a big car
And a photographer pausing
For a newsprint epitaph.

And so on

It's a habit one grows into
Unwittingly at first, then wittily

To hide behind, to cover up,
A nicely English etcetera

To survive a revolution
By painting orchids prettily

A brush-stroke here, downwards,
Dividing subtly into segments

One hesitates to be definite
And then one weeps, and so on.

Variation on an old Chinese theme

A first-world exile
From the third world exiled
To a paper side-chamber
Of the modern Middle Kingdom

Sees the slant-eyed moon
Through a blaze of brandy
And looks south, like a partridge
Knowing only one way to go –

But there's no flight home
(Street-gangs on the pavements
Wolves in the jewellery shops
Police with shotguns in the woods

And history tilting);
Night-flowers scent the air –
I lift my glass to exile.
A shadow joins my table.

Hong Kong Portraits

The economist

Alienated but content, my friend –
The bearded American from Princeton
And San Francisco – sits drinking beer
On the verandah, and talks about Marx
And the Christians. The paradox of love
Lies in its apprehension of objects:
He sees friends as clearly as he loves them –
The banker, for instance, in the circles
Of hell and monopoly, is himself
Exploited by wealth and worldly mansions.
No doubt un-Marxist and un-Godly me
He knows as God's unwilling servant.
The dialectic of mind and charity
Is resolved in the cool winter sunshine.
There is history, too, but that comes later.

The writer

He drinks only soda with ice. 'My name
Is Derek; I am an alcoholic.'
Born in England ('I'm not Austrylian'),
Lived in Sydney, Beirut, Malta, London,
Saigon, Hong Kong, Vancouver – elsewhere too,
Forgotten. Been bombed in a paddy-field,
And bombed almost everywhere, seeing things
Which were not there, and too many which were.
Dragged up his son, drowned in a swimming-pool,
In another country, so kept moving,
With the Furies travelling too, hardly
Behind him. His novels are profligate,
Darkly humorous, richly unhappy,
And they do not stay too long, anywhere;
His heroes end up dead, and his readers
Shake in their arm-chairs, with fear and laughter.

The headmaster (a self-portrait)

He's old enough now to be very pleased
When flatterers say that he looks too young
To be a headmaster. He is afraid
Of heights, revolution, opposition,
Spiders, caves, and almost anything else
You or he can imagine. He is tall
And carries the country of his childhood
On his shoulders, but not in his accent.
Arrogant man, he tends to fall asleep
At his desk, at dinner, or in meetings,
Even sometimes when he should be teaching.
Beneath arrogance waits the Ragged Man,
The stranger, the one-eyed limping Threatener,
With cudgels and curses. You could call it
His fear, or merely his knowing a job
Must be done before the final darkness
Comes clattering down, like small stones and mud
On a coffin, but not in Africa.

Illegal immigrants

Walking on the hillside behind Stanley
We found them – five young men, all dressed oddly
And frightened. We thought they must be students
Till they begged for food, using sign-language.
The children ran to the car without asking
And brought back oranges and biscuits, all
That was left of the picnic. The hungriest
(Or the least frightened) gestured at the sun
To show its movements and then held up four
Thin fingers to show days without eating.
He also gestured us to telephone,
Wrote the number down on an old packet
And, as we left, held his hands to his heart
Like a dancer, to show us that he loved us
Or whoever would answer loved him too.
In the car, I crumpled up the packet.
No one asked any question. I noticed
Our eldest, the tough one, the ruffian,
Hid his face carefully at the window.
I want this poem to be plain and simple.

Ah Chan

The most unservile of servants, Ah Chan,
Speaks a language without past or future,
Even though she was given away, aged two,
By her mother to a cousin. She loves
Her country but not to live there: 'much poor',
She tells me firmly, grinning skinnily.
On Sundays she visits Elder Sister
Who married Big Money, lives on the Peak,
And tries to send her home with the chauffeur;
But Ah Chan travels by bus. For Christmas
She gives us gifts like a vase, a purple
Tree-trunk thing with pandas climbing the stem,
Unbreakable, unhideable. God knows
What she thinks of the things we find for her;
She's far too polite to comment, either way.
She makes me feel like a new arrival,
Not just in China, but on earth; it's true,
Of course, when you measure time by China.

Woo Sam

Something got left out when they made him. Now
He's a talking head on a thin bundle
Of crooked sticks, a puppet with the strings
Tangled forever, a grotesque cartoon
By a sinister god. Strapped in his chair
In the home for spastics, he observes
The important visitors, and later tells
His therapist, 'The tall one was afraid
To look at me, Woo Sam, in my wheel-chair.'

God's own critic

This large lady lays out the Jewish dead.
Her father did too; so would have his son
If he'd had one. Instead, the girl took on
This final office of fidelity
To all-comers, friends and fellow-strangers,
Drowned by accident or drugged on purpose,
Died in their season or well after it,
The cancelled children, and the cancerous,
The awe-stricken ones, and the thankful.

Ireland bred her, Shanghai added interest.
Her husband, the White Russian, whom I call
(Jestingly) Oscar X. Vladivostok,
Brought her here to this temporary island –
And now her children look only to Israel;
And what can she do? She's a homeless one,
Despite the large car, and the five servants –
But she's not complaining: she has her friends,
And her husband, and her duties. Who's complaining?
The world spends too much of its time complaining –
About what, I ask you? We have our health,
And we're not poor, and the children visit.
God has been good, I tell you, recently.

God, you are reproved with that 'recently',
For having shut your eyes to the suffering
Of her generation. And so she wipes
Their poor dead bodies down, and plugs the holes,
And makes the most of what is left to see.
She hopes one day to have it done for her,
And not to be bulldozed into a grave.

M.

Not in our usual circle, of course, he
(Nicknamed 'God' or 'the mad Scot') was inclined
To be high-handed; habits of command
Engraved the face from brow to jaw, and he
Cut short conversation. The Chinese loved him
Because he loomed, towered, lowered, and could burn
The rust off old iron without trying.
Hearing a drunk G.I.S. man slanging
The 'bloody Chinks and their cheating', he told
An underling hovering: 'Sack that man'.
And he did. Yet the Governor would sit
For hours through interminable debate
Without stirring (or sleeping), and focus
Half a life-time in one well-turned phrase.
Except the worst should somehow be better,
And the better no worse than necessary,
One does not care to be too much surprised
By a Governor, nor by a Government.
Laws are not made only to be broken
Nor does repugnance welcome refugees
From the creation of new liberty –
Little else we can serve but our own time,
And a few well-tried certainties:
The best borders need the closest guardians,
And decency becomes our colony.
If something isn't broken, why mend it?

The property millionaire

They're very easy to hate, in the abstract:
Gross fat men, rubbing their hands in the blood
Of workers, pushing prices up and down
For the millions they don't need or deserve.
I met one, in a box at the races,
A wizened old chap, who talked about painting
For nearly an hour; he'd bought a Picasso,
The sketch of a woman, kneeling, naked –
It was worth being rich, he said, to own it
And, when he outlined her shape with his hands,
For a moment I almost believed him.

Group portrait, with cameras

They are gathered on a bare mountain-top,
Grouped, after lunch, for a photograph.
They are teasing the photographer
(Inveterate snapper of holiday shots)
By raising their various cameras
To catch her catching their wind-swept poses
Between rucksacks, sandwiches and beer-cans.
The actual is rather like prose, the poem
Like the absent photographer, who stood
(I remember) on the crumbling granite
Above them, bare-legged and beautiful.
The poem is seen in the lens of the prose,
In the click of her momentary stillness.

The schoolmaster

Like a stork, someone said, watching him run.
Exactly so: the feet placed precisely,
The long thin legs, the stoop, the beaky nose,
A tendency to flap his arms out wide,
A watchful concentration fixed ahead
To make quite sure that nothing moved at all
Which should not move.
                              The world was better once.
Things of course are never what they seem to be,
But what they seemed was easier to bear
In our fathers' time, and when the monarchs
Truly ruled. Unruly's now the word –
Elizabethan cadence, but he thinks
They may have had it right, all right.
                              Dear friend,
They may not always like you much, right now;
But you're the one they'll come to show their wives –
The boys I mean – and whom they'll think of, when
(Old men and full of tales) they want to tell
Just how it was, way back in the old days:
Like a stork he looked, with his long thin legs
And a huge beaky nose, and a temper.
You knew exactly where you stood with him –
He never said a thing you could not trust.

The world was better in those older days.

Love & Death in Cape Town

i.m. Simon Driver, 1941–87

Don't fuss

'The doctors have told me,' my brother wrote,
'There is little else they can do for me –
So I shall accept your invitation
(If I may)' – and so he came to visit,
Kom kuier, in the language of childhood
We still use, because it's our own country
Where I have made a very private peace,
Though only for dying.
                                        One-legged, breathless,
As bald as an old man from the chemo
(Not to mention the cobalt, nor the scars
Where the surgeons had cut the bits they could)
He told my children things I'd forgotten
Entirely, but remembered as he told,
Like meeting someone after a long time
Who had once been quite familiar –
That I had held a stone in my right hand
So I could turn that way on dismissal
From parade – I've never known left from right –
How I had frowned with such ferocity
That my nickname had been Old Baboon Eyes –
How I'd lined up shoes on a bedroom sill
To fire at the guinea-fowl machine-gunning
In the dawn – oh, so many stories
Of all the years we gave away to time –
And then he'd cough: and cough, and cough, and cough,
Until we'd hold our breath and look away,
Or offer him a drink, or call the doc –
And he'd whisper, 'Don't fuss,' and then he'd cough
Until we thought the scars would have to burst.
But we couldn't fuss, because he said so.

Both he and I knew well, but didn't say,
That when our father died, from a bad heart,
His last words as he lay on the sofa
While my brother sat next to him waiting
And could see what was happening but knew
There was nothing he could do, nor doctors,
Nor the ambulance men, nor hospitals,
Nor the priest next door – nothing, nothing to do
But wait – and, waiting, my father whispered
That last invincible chorus to death:
'Don't fuss.'
        And then he said, 'I think you should …
You know … come home. They'd let you in, for me,
I think. Come home. I'd like it very much.'

Grace and Silence

I thought his name was Silas: it suited
Since he collected junk of any kind
And stored it where my brother didn't keep
His car: junk of any kind – half a bike;
Old magazines; a broken saw; a lid
Without a pan; a handless clock; a lamp
My brother'd thrown away; broken glasses;
Cheque book stubs; shelves of any size;
All my brother's left-foot shoes. ('I s'pose,'
My brother said, 'there may be someone else
Who's lost the other leg, and needs those shoes –
Ol' Silas would find him.') He packed it up,
The junk I mean, in huge cardboard parcels
And monthly shipped them back, to the homeland,
Victorian dealer, Miser, Silas,
Quaint and kindly …

'But you've got it wrong,'
My brother said. 'His name isn't Silas –
Silence, that's his name – parents called him that,
In hope he might have been, or since he was,
Like Ruth, I guess, or Hope, or Charity.'
Silence collected junk, for which he found
A use. Silence was always there. Silence
Took care. Silence shook hands and said, warmly,
'So you're the big brother, come from England,
Principal, of a high school, Simon said.'
(Not 'my baas', I was pleased to hear –
'I said he couldn't clean my car if he
"Baas"ed me,' my brother said, sotto voce.)
'I am very pleased to meet,' Silence said –
And I was very glad I'd left my bags inside.

Grace, on the other hand, came on Tuesdays
To do the ironing, and clean the flat
(Which needed it by then, I tell you man!).
She borrowed next week's wage to pay the school

Her children wouldn't go to, but he kept
A month or two ahead, and then forgot,
Although he said, 'I think she adds it up, and pays
In overtime.' He wasn't sure. 'Who cares?'
He said. 'It's just a kind of grown-up game
Between the three of us. When Silence needs
A bit of *geld*, he cleans my car, then says
"I cleaned your car because it needed me" –
It's a kind of local truce we've made,
I guess. I give them what they want, and they
Protect me, for a little time at least.
That's all I need, you see.'

                    Grace and Silence:
Grace does the dishes; Silence keeps the door.

Aubade

A pre-recorded priest awoke me
Who stayed in bed and did not climb the stairs
Of the tower I could not quite see there
Somewhere towards the Cape Town end of Mowbray;
And I remembered other dawns I'd heard
All those years before, in this fated town –
And most of all a friend who woke me up
To come to celebrate his first son's birth –
And we heard the muezzin sing, over Wynberg.
The ghosts of all the slaves who'd built the house
Were gathered round. 'Champagne for sons,' we said,
And 'Freedom in our time.' The old house cheered.

That son's a scion of the further Left
In London now; his father somewhere else
High-up now, one hears; and I am teaching
Clever boys in Berkhamsted. We've grown up –
And some of us have grown away, and some
Are dead, and some will die, and soon, I fear.
The dawn-song blares; the curtains pulse with wind;
The shutters bar the early light. How strange,
How strange it is to be alive, and back
Where I belonged so much, now not at all.

Recognition

I did, I confess, grow sometimes weary:
Dying takes so long, so many trunk calls
And cheerful letters, so many alarms
And long waiting, old *Saries* and *Digests*
In antiseptic waiting-rooms, aglow
With brave aftershave and nurses rustling.
In the Cancer Outpatients, Kronald's 'firm',
Where I wheeled you, for once in a chair
Though you kept the crutches close, since you could,
If you needed to, walk on your own – 'hell,
I've only lost a leg, not all my brain' –
We saw the old white-haired Congress man, come
(I guess) for a check-up or an X-ray,
Or was it a diagnosis of death?
Grizzled and fit, in charge of his body,
In the way you sometimes get disciplined
In a cell, with certainty of triumph,
And structured hours of careful exercise,
He sat waiting, as he was now used to,
With a fat white warder, spinnaker guts
And a *bokbaard* not quite hiding the chin –
And the shirt-sleeved man with a holster gun
Under his armpit, by the eyes SB
If cold counts any more, who looked at me
As if he half-remembered who I was –
As I did him, all right, standing in my cell
To say, 'We'll get you bastards, every one …'
And now he slightly frowned, and I wondered
If he wondered what I was doing there …

And the old black man stared me through as if …
As if I was just another white man
Waiting for death, in J7, Groote Schuur.

66

Marginal Miranda

Last time I saw Miranda was in Kings –
The inner quad where dwell the dons – but she,
Poor girl, was fat: the spuds had done her in
And filled her out, not merely plump – dumpling:
A suet girl, as fat as Cambridge pie.
I'd known her twenty years; she used to pass
For white, a tiny, silken, dark-eyed dart
(Treble-twenty!). Though it did not touch her brain
To see her fat was just a little sad,
Even in Cambridge, and even in Kings,
Though it's some way to go from District Six.
Now, in Cape Town, I had to ask her name:
'Is that …?'
           'Yes, it is,' my sister said,
And my brother said, 'Too thin', reproving.
'She came back?' I asked, amazed. She came back.
Heads were shaken. It was England, or cold,
Or breakdown, or the usual masculine
Antic, something like that. I heard her say
To a man who'd trapped her in a corner,
'Yes, I'm a librarian', and she added –
Like a huge brass name-plate – 'from Grassy Park'.
Coloureds live in Grassy Park, never whites;
You cannot pass for white in Grassy Park.
So coming back was more than just a change
Of scene or style. She had moved centre-page,
Marginal Miranda. She was what she was;
She did not merely seem. I didn't see
Who drove her home, so asked; my brother said,
'She went by bus, early; she always does.'

Old friend

for Maeder Osler

And after twenty years apart, old friend –
Best friend, best man, and my best defender
In those bad days of nineteen-sixty-four
(My father dead, my girl-friend gone, and half
My friends in gaol, or run away abroad) –
How good it is to find you now at last
Restored to where you started from, and set
On rich well-watered land, between koppies.
May droughts stay well away from all your lands,
Guerrilla fighters not descend this route
From north to south; and may your broad shoulders
Not carry more than proper for a man
Who never tried to shirk the heaped-up guilt
Of all those generations buried there
Below the copse. We fought well in those days,
But now our choices hardly multiply.
We live with what we are, the one choice left
To leave or not: I did, and you did not.
What else to say? Across a brandy bottle
Empty now, you raise an empty glass
And grin at me: 'Eh, man, I tell you what –
Twenty years is but a blink of the eye.'

The advocaat

Fiction couldn't bear him: he is too odd
To be easily believed in – a Buddhist
And not merely a monk but an abbot
And in California, now returned
To the fatherland because he desires
Possessions: a suit or two, a small house,
A wife and some children. So in chambers
Next to the Hanging Court of the Eastern Cape
He holds temporary sway, and defends
Scarred revolutionaries and scared children.
Who was it made the pattern? Who broke it?
There are different roads to the one river.

The man outside the Supreme Court

Above the polished shoes the polished gun:
Above the light blue shirt the pale blue eyes.

Well, goodbye

I'd been skirting it all day, what I'd say
At our last parting, at the aerodrome
(Our joking way of sharing older times
To use the older terms gone out of taste).
Of course we knew. At lunch I said something
Rather feeble about the next summer
(Already I had shifted hemispheres
And meant the summer on the northern side).
Of course we knew. This was to be our last
Goodbye. There would be no more coming back.
We've always hated partings, kept them brief,
Said, 'Well, goodbye', quickly touched, turned and walked –
And don't look back.
                    And don't look back. And that
Was what we did; habit saved us from grief,
At least in public. It'd been just the same
Leaving home for boarding school, the long wait
On the hot platform, parents standing there,
And nothing left to say, not even
Silly things like, 'Now don't forget to write'.
We used to say to them, 'Goodbye and go.
We're on the train, leaving any moment now.
Why wait? Why drag this parting out? We don't
Want to go away – you know. Any moment now
Mom will cry. Please go. Just say goodbye'.

The night he died, before I heard the news,
I woke at three, in a far country, far
Even from England. I had had a dream.
I often dreamed of him, my small brother
With cancer, though never dead. But this time
He was dead. I was sure. I woke in tears.
He'd come to me, as ghost, or something else,
To let me know, with gruff laconic words:
'So this is where you are: in India …
I thought I'd better let you know. I'm off …'
And then, as usual, flatly, 'Well, goodbye'.

And I woke up, in grief but also joy,
Since wordless Simon had to go like that –
And going thus meant something else than death;
And I thought: but no one will believe this –
I should wake my hosts to say, 'My brother's dead;
I know he's dead', before they telephone –
But I can't wake them now; it's three o'clock.
I'll tell them when we meet for morning tea.
I forgot of course. One does. The call came
At breakfast time.

Home-coming

Of course, one claims to choose. I chose to leave,
Although I called it something else than exile –
Going back, I said, to where we started.
Impressed by light and how it changes north
(The cooler pastel to the vibrant south),
Acclimatised – to foreign manners too –
I lost my accent and I gained a wife.
I became an Englishman – well, nearly ...

And then, as always, came the kindly ones
(One calls them that, old friend; they don't much like
Their other older names). They intimate
Just what we might have been, if things had been
A little different. They take us back
To where we can't forget to be ourselves.
They know exactly what each moment cost.
They spike our hearts on thorns, like butcher-birds.

And so I'm home again, where I began,
And what I lost is what I want to know.
'Yes, I have mellowed, as you said I would' –
Who doesn't, old friend? Now we stand in touch
To watch our sons win caps for teams we cheered
As boys, and late at night we stumble home,
Unhanged, but fat and growing old. How swift
The years run passing by, as fleet as wings!

Inner cities trample outwards, jeering.
Someone else a little like me thought, once,
He knew his mind, who claimed he made a choice.
And I sat in a Cape Town train in tears
(In public mark you) and a mild old man
In a facing seat said softly, *No one*
Blames you. Did he know who I was? He did –
He was myself in thirty years or so.

The more we learn about the kindly ones,
Old friend, the more ourselves they seem to be:
Hell isn't other people – hell is ourselves,
To be trapped for ever in might-have-been
And as-you-were, like driving down a motorway
For ever and ever at the same speed
In the same lane with the same lights blinking
On the same wet surface, always oneself …

What we are, old friend, is very flimsy,
Flesh or even less than that. We die
Before we hardly breathe, but all the same
These nicely English hesitations seem
A cold reaction. Queues of ancient guilt
Lengthen. Have you seen children starve? Or faced
Rifles held by angry, frightened conscripts?
But who aged forty-six throws stones at tanks?

Well, someone does, old son. They sweat in gaol,
Suspended upside down, on 'trapezes',
Or shriek between the plus and minus signs,
Some of those I knew a hundred years ago;
And one was murdered at his own front door.
The policeman stares across the desk at me
And calls me sir; I smile politely back
(And once these bastards were afraid of me).

I make excuses: age, and England. The real
Remains, although I'd wish it otherwise.
Burning tyres are the latest weaponry,
Called 'necklaces'. One must believe in change,
But this is nothing soon to what will come.
Who mans the road-blocks is uncertain
And death-squads police the unmade streets.
The missing faces crowd around our graves.

The Journey Back

'The Department has decided to remove the restrictions placed upon you.'

SAA 230: Mission statement

What happens next may justify the past:
What happened then must be retrieved.
                  I write
On a long flight from England, home again,
Not sure of what I'll find, not sure of self,
Not sure of anything, I guess – pretence
Apart. In Godel's Proof: the things that are
Contain their own construction. Disproof
Of what the place may wish to prove untrue:
Untruth of what the place may prove.
                  I live
A long away; I'm not me now; I'm not.
The language knows so much beyond oneself …
No time returns, but places comes again.
The fiscal shrike, the butcher-bird, jackie
Hangman, spiked my heart on thorns; but now
Here I am at home again – or what was home
And may no longer be, as we drop down
Into the golden town, Johannesburg –
And at the entry desk I hesitate,
Come back an Englishman: which queue to choose
I know quite well, but still resent the sign
Which tells me what I am and what I was.
So this is hell, I think, where I've returned –
Who chooses what he hates and what hates him?
And then, in the Arrivals Hall, smiling you,
My oldest friend, the one who doesn't change –
Except a little bit for time and age,
Just about enough to keep things decent –
And this is never hell, this is my home
Come round again, like an undying spring.

Mid-winter here, I note.
                              To journey thus,
I now set out – I now set down – I laugh,
I cry, I hold my breath, I peer for ghosts,
I see no ghosts but hear their every word.
This egocentric exercise in verse
I dedicate to people whom I've loved:
You, and you, and you. I shall not name you,
A single one; you must guess, my dears, and smile
At hints and half-suggestions nudged abroad
As now I nudge these fledgelings from the page
To try their best in all that enormous air.

Chai Mani Mani: And no sign of rain

Sun on the far hills, on the near plain
     And no sign of rain –
Lichen on grey stones, orange and white
     Imprinted in light.

Cloud over the hills, shading the plain
     But no sign of rain –
Repeated prints on the dusty track
     As it doubles back.

The cold wind cranking the windmill round
     With a dried-up sound –
The leopard patterns the path again:
     And no sign of rain.

Uplands School, White River: Elegy

I found the road, and then the turning right
Just past the second dam, and up the hill –
    The floating trees were there, still –
    The valley dropping out of sight,

The red-earth drive rising to the big house
Set firm in solid white against the sky:
    The school my father left, to die
    Ten days later, in a strange place.

I stopped the car to hold the moment thus,
To see the things that had or hadn't changed,
    The lawns and gardens re-arranged,
    The classrooms added to the house,

The way the trees had grown, shrinking distance.
Once, this was my home, and it isn't now.
    I turn to show my daughter how
    The shape of things has altered since.

It made me catch my breath to see the known
Unchanged, and yet I hardly knew a face;
    Strange to be a stranger in a place
    Which once had seemed so much my own.

A grave-eyed child is brought to say hullo.
I have to ask again the name I thought
    I heard, and heard all right: I taught
    Her father thirty years ago,

When mine was ill and – too briefly – I returned.
I should have stayed; instead I went away
    To where I thought my duty lay.
    You died then, when my back was turned.

I knew quite well I wouldn't see you here
But nonetheless I guess I hoped to learn
    Miraculous on my return
    That we had somehow skipped the years

And when I'd seen the hall they built to mark
Your name and years of service here, I took
    Myself away alone to look
    At where I knew you'd be at work

If you were here at all. For sure it's you
I came to see, and really nothing else.
    In that dark house no shadow falls
    Across the threshold. That's not you

Ghostly at the desk. That's me. That damned pipe
And those long nights of sharpened pencils, soon
    And sooner took you off too young –
    And almost all that's left is hope

That we might meet on the last busy day –
If such a day there is. And I despair
    As I stare out of doors to where
    I hear the latest children play:

There is no God, there is no life to come,
There is no time when we shall meet again:
    We have to learn to live with pain,
    Impermanence and our long home.

And as I stood in blank-eyed misery there
Reflecting on my father who was dead,
    My daughter took my arm and said,
    'I thought that I might find you here.

'You've come to look for him, I know. I told
The others where you'd be. It's just like you.
    I wish that I could meet him too.
    I want a father when I'm old.'

Nieu Bethesda: The Owl House

If I had a gun, Koos, I'd shoot myself.
                    —Helen Martins

Instead, she waited till he'd gone away
And then she swallowed caustic soda.
In hospital, she took three days to die.

Ground glass in her eyes was the first wounding;
The next was crippled hands. And people talked ...
Perhaps it's best to choose the time oneself.

Someone took the money which she'd put away.
The Persian rug went next, the good table,
The crimson lamps. The glass-eyed owls stare still

From their wire cage, and fragmented glass glints
On every wall and chair: if we could have
Enough of light, if we could have enough

Of time, there'd be no need for hate or haste.
The concrete pilgrims raise their heads and hands;
A sign says East, but never where it was.

Mermaids call the geese to come, but no one
Fills the pool for them these days. I have seen
The future, and I fear it's mainly dust.

The Valley of Desolation: Once

Notice: *Do not even think of throwing stones.*

I thought I might have found the perfect place:
It went awry, or had been all along.
It seems as if a builder started here
To make a desert temple out of stone
And then got bored. Great rocks are piled
On lesser rocks, and upward stacked like years
In crazy thoughts of history.
                                        I thought
I'd learn at least to live with what I found
Intolerable, but could not keep my peace.
I tried to get away with thinking things
Illegal. I was wrong. The state demands
One's heart and head … So next I raised my hands
In supplication or despair, but found
Surrender meant one's soul. One goes away.
One's not afraid to say. One needs to keep
One's private counsel. And one doesn't judge.

It has its own magnificence, to fail
In such a large-scale way. The view from here
Goes all the way to where the desert ends
In light refracted through the very edge
Of sun obscured by mountains.
                                        One forgets
The scale of things.
                          It's strange to lose one's past
And then to get it back again.
                                        There's little new
In exile: we've done it all the time, you see;
Emperors are the same, whichever view
They take of history. They build these cities
Which then fall down. And Nature does the same,
Just a bit more slowly. It's no surprise
To find oneself now gazing down a gorge
And keeping well away.

One's learned to cope.
It's turned out well. The sell-by date is passed,
But once again one is the man one was,
Or so they say who know me best of all.
I'm far too old to go around again.
The point of 'Once' is once.
                              And then one's dead.

Uniondale: National Anthem

Heaven's blue, deep-sea,
And distant dustlands:
Bodies in stairwells,
Silence in police-cells –
These are not talking.

Summer's heat, pale-sky,
And dust storms rising:
Crowds on the highway
Drunk before noonday –
This looks like weeping.

The mountain's on fire,
Smoke against skyline:
Darkens the daylight
Emptying foresight –
Guests should bring rifles.

Sudden dusk, downfall
Sunglow deepening:
Lights on the roadside
Flare up the hillside –
The future's arrived.

Storms River: Chaos theory

I watch the winter waves all day
To guess the place they'll start to gather up
And lift, and lift so slowly to the cusp
    Which hangs a moment as it breaks
In sudden downward curve of lighter green
    Before the backward spray of spume
        Which tags the wave
    Appends a rainbow briefly to its edge.

Though gravity has not yet trapped
The further stars in ordered evidence
(For light allows I may not see them now
    Where curves the fleeting universe)
This random music in my head includes
    The rainbow, cusp and spray,
        The light and stars,
The wave's return, the certain night to come.

The Wilderness: Written on water

The sheen of dying wind
Across the lake –
The darkling light
As light delights the air
(The language knows so much beyond oneself)

The web of weaving wind
Across the lake –
The water light
Of silver shining air
(The language knows so much beyond oneself)

We think of something lost
In writing down
The flux of time:
But what completes our thought?
(The language knows so much beyond oneself)

The thread of meaning lost
In noting down
That fleeting time:
Precise the moment caught
(The language knows so much beyond oneself).

Cape Nowhere: Cranes

On a wide plain, the blue cranes are displaying, oh so sedately,
As if at a Regency ball, too languid for passion, too bored
To fight for favours, for why be bothered when one's so elegant?
They break from the dance to bow to someone they presume
      they know
(But how can you tell, these days?) or to pick a stray delicacy
From the tray of a supine servant. You see, one could (if one wished
Or if the occasion served) pick a fight, provoke an incident
Or make love, my dearest, in whatever order you like, my dear,
My dear, step step step step bow
                step step step
                              bow
                                    step,

                              step step step bow.

Breede River: Appearances

I

The names reveal what must have been:
Olifantsrivier, Elandsvlei,
Bontebokkloof and Wydgeleë,
Buffelsvlakte and Heuningspruit.
On maps and signs they teem, which now
Lie empty. On roadsides only
The flowers grow which once fed herds
And more. The ostrich fans his wings
As if there were no fence to leap:
He wears his kingdom in his head
That now is given up for good;
The names reveal what it's become:
Verlatenheid, Bittervlakte,
Vergenoeg, Verkeerdevlei,
Putsonderwater, Kaallaagte,
Droëpit, Jammerdrif, Omdraaisvlei.

II

The river's broad enough; the silt
Is swept aside in tides of rain
From where the river doesn't end.
You look from here to far inland
And mountains edged in cloud, to see
What judgements cannot pass, the trees
Like liver-spots on old men's hands.

III

We took a boat upstream to find
A peaceful shore to picnic on.
Close up, the grass was really swamp,
The sandy cove a mire of mud,
And wind between the gasps of sun
A cold reminder that we knew
Too well. Flamingos, avocets,
Darters, stilts, spoonbills, ibises,
Hamerkops, spur-winged geese, in flocks
Would move a sand-bank further on
If we went up too close, or fly
In noisy circles back again
To nearly where they'd been before.

IV

Returning, by the other shore,
We saw the seal – outlawed ancient –
Who'd made that stretch of river his:
Up popped his head, like an old bather,
Bald and whiskered, but sleek and fit,
To eye these odd intruders here,
And then was gone and stayed away
Although we hoped – and waited ...

V

Beyond the surf, the wintering whales,
Oil-black and tumbling huge, with calves
Kept close, scraps of white between the bulk,
Impossible to count, the flukes
And spouts and snouts and jumbled tails –
But gathered underneath that sky
And timeless in the swells, returned
Each year for year on year, as if
There were no time at all, no loss
Where out beyond the headlands wait
Harpoons, and ropes, and sharpened knives.

Stellenbosch: Back in the labyrinth

All those years ago, I knew so much.
I know so little now. Am entirely
In this ignorance. Am so replete
Of flatulent uncertainty. Am
Hardly a person now, more a bag
Of guts and small circles, of histories
Not written down and now half-forgotten.
So, when I turn a corner, and meet you
With a similar stiff-kneed, shambling gait
And the slow staring just above one's head,
Such yellow-green of eyes, and heavy jaw,
Cut of chin and slant of eyes, and I say:
'Why, it's me! I haven't changed at all:
How odd to meet me now, so many years
Since last we talked, and what I want to know
Is what you've done, what honours gained, and when,
Where you live, what children, wife and job …?'
And then I thought it couldn't be, not me,
Not all that time ago, and not this place.
It must be someone else, a nicer man,
A cousin's son, or some ancestral jape
Who doubled back to catch me unawares
And say: I thought I'd meet you here, in time …
He looked straight through, as if he wasn't me
At all, was just a nasty thought of age
And lanky, sagging corpulence, come back
From overseas, and clearly not much use
In any way which counts, in this labyrinth.
Was it he who dropped the string, or me?
Am I the beast who roars forlornly thus
Between the high walls, in the dark stable?

St James: Incomplete story

And so, later, I walked down the hill from Seaforth to take the train back from Simon's Town, thinking that I did not want to walk the whole way but, at Kalk Bay, just past the harbour, with the tide in and the wind blowing, I remembered the family story that on the night I was born my father had walked from Mowbray to Fish Hoek where he had lived with his mother, brother and sisters, and then home again to the news that my mother was well and I alive – unlike the child before me which my mother had miscarried at six months; so I got down from the train at St James to walk, suddenly remembering a girl I had loved who lived above the beach at St James with her sister and widowed father – who had not much approved of a tall and skinny suitor with no money and strange ideas about politics – though that was no drawback when it came to first love, especially as we walked, danced and held hands to the singing of Frank Sinatra, jazzily syncopated, the rhythm of the sung melody *lento lugubre* stretching most longingly each side of the rhythm of the big band, like embroidery counterpointed on a coat blowing in the wind ... *And every time I look at you/I'm such a happy in-di-vid-ual* ... There was a new path on the sea side of the railway line, carefully cemented across the rocks; the tide was still coming in, the wind blowing inland from False Bay, and the waves broke high, soaking the path and beyond, until eventually even the most cautious walker was so wet with salt-spray that it seemed hardly worth going on, or for that matter back ...

On Noordhoek beach

The same old beach. A windy day, and plumes
Of froth flick off the dumpers twisting round.
Like seals, the wet-suited surfers catch a breath
Before the seventh wave, and upwards climb
The double-handed kites, while casual gulls
Saunter in the pools as if they owned the place.

Our party's broken up: one's run ahead
For half a mile, one's fallen fast asleep
Just where a dune deflects the cold, and two
Are walking on the edge of broken waves.
That leaves me, and I can't make up my mind.
I'm trapped between the beach and sun, the wind
And waves, the angry kites and passive gulls:
To come or go, to walk or run, to sleep
Or wake. Marauding dogs come barking past,
Their tails like tattered sails on Chinese junks –
And if I stand here long enough, perhaps
The wind will blow me back again to where
I was when last I waited on this beach.

Langa: i.m. Ernest Galo

Driving past this township on a cold day
In August, with the mist down on the sea,
I wonder who else now will remember
Ernest Galo: the girl who seemed too young
To be a wife? The gang who drank with us?
Some clerk with a long nose in police files?
Those days it was a crime enough to talk
And student leaders were important men
With big ideas: our anger and laughter
Were tracers without bullets to the days
When guns would not rule us. We offended:
The policemen came in the morning to wake us;
He fled across the border to safety.
The small pain in his right side festered fast
And, when the doctors flew him back again,
It was too late. Still, just in case, the police
Arrested the body.
            At the funeral
In Langa, there was no room in the church;
Five thousand, someone said, but who counted?
And all black, except two. We all walked past
The open coffin, where a rotten job
Had been done with white powder and make-up –
And I looked twice, in hope of a mistake.
We shook hands with the old parents, the bride,
The padre in his surplice, and then stood
Around the house while the police kept a threat
Of armour not completely out of sight. And then
Came the speeches, in Xhosa and English –
The grand old man of the Cape ANC
(So old he wore a frock coat and striped trousers)
Spoke of the new Africa coming soon
(Though this was Langa and the days were bad) –
And there were others, whom I forget now ...
And then the family called me to speak:
Clapping hands opened a way to where
The microphone was placed, on the front path

To the small house where Ernest Galo lay
Dead, aged twenty-five. The man beside me
Translated each phrase, so I had time
To ponder; but the far words won't return,
Just the smell of dust under a cold sky,
And the policemen circling, not out of sight,
The crowd listening, and then joining in,
And the small sound of a wife's weeping.

One could leave it there, I guess: his young wife
Could be the main thing worth remembering.
But thirty years have gone and now I need
Another speech for the quiet people.
One owes to them to be at last honest,
And to him too, I guess, thirty years dead.

Of the bigger deaths one may make some sense:
The court-room speech, the heroic gesture,
The mad assault on the armed enemy,
Even the death 'while trying to escape'
Or the falling from torturers' windows.
No deaths are small, but there are accidents
As there might have been when one lobbed a grenade
Through the window of the house with children asleep.
So I mourn your death now, Ernest Galo,
And hope the world may remember you now
For courage, fidelity and laughter.
What one wants is mercy, not sacrifice.

Botterkloof Pass: Threnody in the mountains

i.m. Graham Vinicombe Wincester Clowes,
Lt 1st Battalion Gordon Highlanders
Killed 30 Jan 1901

I wonder where the sniper lay
Who blew this breath-child clean away

And whether, when the work was done,
He rode for home, and kissed his son,

Or boasted of his aim that day,
Uphill and ninety yards away.

The only grave for miles around,
The frontier wind the only sound.

And what his people thought when they
Came each year to watch and pray,

To lay their flowers on his grave,
To keep the little left to save.

Romantic nonsense to suppose
Some English ghost may here repose.

And yet I want us all to weep
For such a boy so long asleep.

Oorlogskloof

The others go too near the edge.
This is Oorlogskloof
Where the San were slaughtered:
The old men, the old women,
The young men, the young women,
The children, their mothers, their fathers,
The pubescent girls
The adolescent boys
The priests
The artists, the song-makers and the trackers
Carvers of arrowhead and knobkerrie
And those who knew how to talk to the Dutch farmers.

Since no one owns the land or the cattle
The San steal. They also fall down dancing
When the sounding stones are pounded with stones,
And the stones make the brain's music inside.
They talk to eland
As eland talk to elephants
They read the wind
They see a lizard hiding ten yards away
They are not to be trusted
They hide among rocks
And they know as much about poison as cobras.

So the Dutch farmers drove them like monkeys
Into this canyon without an outlet
And then killed them one by one, as they stepped
Toward the waterfall which not even
The San could climb. No one counted the dead.
And when the last old woman had been dragged
From behind the rocks
And her throat cut
And the last baby thrown against a rock face
The Dutchmen went away
To their homesteads, churches, wives and children.
The guns were primed to deal with the next species.

Our guide tells us he hears their ghosts sometimes
When he hunts what little is left down there:
Dassies, duikers, baboons. Leopards? we ask.
No leopards, he's certain. No, no leopards –
Only the ghosts of the San still retreating
When the hot wind blows along Oorlogskloof.

Namaqualand: Sorcerer's song

Being so tall, I see
From odd angles:
Thus it was I saw those paintings
High in the secret caves.

Young girls dancing I saw
Oddly angled:
Rain from a sky without clouds
And flowers appearing.

Being so old, I know
Most of the words:
Thus it was I heard voices
From those vacant spaces.

What was said I knew
Without learning:
These were designed for dreaming
In the strangest places.

Sir Lowry's Pass

Where the wagon passed
Rocks were scarred;
Here the dead were laid,
Peace was made.

Here a childhood passed
Slow as days;
Here ill-fortune came
All the same.

Where the earth is burned
Proteas grow;
Like the summer grass
All things pass.

Here the past came back
Clearly named:
Here the years are paid,
Grief is stayed.

L'Envoi: Hauts Champs: The blessing

Suddenly, then, in the garden, I saw
The familiar tufted head, fanned out,
Flaunting his panache like an old school tie.

I've forgotten who told me the story.
The bird flew like words when I spoke too loud:
'Look! It's a hoopoe. He's come to bless us.'

The silence after the end's not the same
As the silence before. From the uplands
Came the ultimate blessing of *Upupa*
Epops: 'hoop hoop hoop hoop.'
                              I say: 'Amen.'

Holiday Haiku

July–August 1996

For my beloved
travelling companion,
with whose eyes I see.

19 July: In transit

Crumpled, crabby, curt,
an air-weary traveller,
lost – like his luggage.

20 July: Avalon (2)

After sudden dusk
sudden silence. The song-birds
abandon the day.

21 July: Southern Cross

Old familiar
returns me to my childhood,
always pointing south.

22 July: Hoopoe

Hoopoe on the lawn
flares his russet black-tipped crest –
exile's home again.

23 July: In a landscape

Empty roads deceive:
paths that circle further hills
circle back again.

24 July: Black school-children

They carry no books
as they run to distant schools:
it's too cold to wave.

24 July: The long road south

Nelspruit, Waterval
Boven, Machadadorp, Volksrust,
Ladysmith, Durban.

28 July: Grahamstown

This is where I start –
but not (thank God) end my days:
unless my luck fails.

29 July: Cape laughing doves

The doves have gathered
this side of the razor wire
on the sunlit path.

1 August: Full moon over Grahamstown

The singular eye
of the night-world, staring down
at new Africa.

4 August: Outeniqua

These are old places:
like newly-washed white hair, clouds
wisp down the mountains.

5 August: The stone guest

The hours bark like dogs;
street-lamps imitate the dawn.
The past shakes the door.

9 August: Man with dog

From the gate he asks:
''n Stukkie brood vi' my hond –
Ek ôk, samblief.'

11 August: Resolution and independence

The old man who sells
wood by the wayside works on,
flailed by the rain-storm.

13 August: Babel

The new spokes-someone
skitters from Afrikaans to …
one's not quite sure what.

14 August: Capetonian

It's a lekker day –
sun mos' shining, win' jus' drop'.
God's in heaven.
Is it?

14 August: Karoo

This hard bare landscape
delights my eyes, lets them stretch
to the horizon.

15 August: Hanglip Farm (1)

Ice on the vlei today,
colder indoors than out:
but all day sunshine.

16 August: The naming

Hanglip, not Hangklip:
the brother who inherited
thought it the worse deal.

6 August: Like sheep to the slaughter

Their legs hobbled tight,
dumped in the bakkie, the sheep
seem to be sleeping.

17 August: Plenty

The rivers flowing,
dams full, and blue cranes dancing
in celebration.

17 August: The long road north

Karoo to Highveld,
on the straight road, the broad way
to Johannesburg.

17 August: Johannesburg Airport

Too many – people,
officials, voices, and signs –
let us go home now.

Requiem

*'For I am a stranger with thee
And a sojourner as all my fathers were
O spare me a little that I may recover my strength
Before I go hence and am no more seen.'*
[Psalm XXXIX]

*'Herr, lehre doch mich, dass ein Ende mit mir haben muss,
und mein Leben ein Ziel hat, und ich davon muss.'*
[Psalm XXXIX, as in Brahms' *German Requiem*, 3rd movement]

Before sunrise

There are ghosts in the garden mists
Like moving statues, or trees on the march,
Or wraiths of seaweed. And there is silence
Like the dead walking in a dream.

I dream constantly of the dead.
Into my sleep they come walking, walking,
In this frozen dark of mid-winter dawn –
The blank-eyed ghosts of Africa.

I peer from my bedroom window,
As if I were a drowned man looking out
At undersea translucence, refracted
Through this awkward English light.

There is no wind, but still the mist
Weaves at random, and seems to make the trees
Step back and forth, side to side, to and fro,
Like crowds before they start a march.

The dead are walking out of sleep,
And once again I see them staring, all
Those seekers from the dark, frozen-faced.
I fear it might be me they want.

This is the child who drowned himself
In half-a-foot of water, this the boy
Who stepped in error from a mountain-side,
Here's one who swallowed drink and pills;

A girl who cut her throat for love;
The man the gun-men got, through his own front door,
And here the one they hanged for planting bombs,
And this the death-cell hero.

And then my own, the ones I love:
My uncles, both killed in the war up north;
My brother, died of cancer, far too soon –
    The friends I lost before their time,

The farmer and the auctioneer,
She who fell to the sea from a great height,
The steady ones who chose to stick things out,
    And those who had no choice at all.

And, most of all, you my father:
I did not think I'd see you walk this path
Out of my dreams, with a stone-set face,
    To chide your son for choosing wrong.

We make the choices that we can,
But make them only once. You too knew that.
I cannot help it if you disapprove.
    It's I who live with what I chose.

Old son, it's Judgement Day at last.
You chose, all right. It's choices that we're here
To judge: I and all the rest. You made them;
    We judge, the dead you answer to.

How whitely glistens the hoar-frost
In lower branches, and how finely spun
The lace on the naked beech and beech-hedge.
    The night is trapped in frozen webs.

The cold is in my bones. The dawn
Lies heavy on the dead flowers and lawns.
The College bells are muffled in the mist;
    I cannot tell which hour they chime.

Behind me someone stirs. It's day,
Or something which approximates. Outside,
The mists retreat, the cars begin, but, still,
    It's time for me to make reply.

This is the beach where I spent my childhood
(Spent my childhood)
This is the house on the beach
I was as free as a sandboy
This is the sea where I swam so bravely
(Swam so bravely)
This is the school where I learned my lessons
(What good teachers)
This is the church where I said my prayers
This is the cell where the policemen held me
(Oh so safely
Oh so safely).

Love-song in twelve fragments

I
In lifts sometimes
I still see dancers
Standing with their feet
At right angles.

II
So short-sighted
Without your glasses
You walked right past me
Because I'd changed shirts.

III
Night-walking
To stand outside
A lighted window
Which may not be yours.

IV
The police-car slows;
The trick is
Not to hesitate.
I always walk this street
At half past three.

V
Long days
On Fourth Beach,
A couple in a coterie,
Brown and skinny
Sleek with sun-oil
Too broke to eat
Not needing to, anyway.

VI

In bed at last, you wept,
But made me go on.

VII

At the railway station
You cried so sadly
I thought at last
You loved me too –
I did not realise
You were crying
For what was passing.

VIII

The last letter my father wrote
Before he died
Was to welcome you
Into the family.

IX

If I'd known then
What I know now
Things might have been
Different –
So one says,
Forgetting one knew then
What one has forgotten now.

X

It took a friend
(Of yours, not mine)
Finally to tell me
I was wasting my time,
And yours, and hers.
I had never liked her.

XI
Sometimes still,
Even after half a lifetime,
Someone's head will turn
In the particular way of dancers,
A fraction slower than the shoulders,
Or a chin will tilt
And short-sighted eyes focus,
And my stolid heart
(In its fashion)
Dances.

XII
In the city,
Kaku, beloved,
Raining.

'I shall keep my mouth as it were with a bridle.'

[Psalm XXXIX]

For a time, it seemed thoroughly the best thing
To keep my mouth shut. I looked to the dead
To be my judges, since what they had said
Made so much more sense than the immediate.

I said I believed in God, but my God
Was a version of justice. I cried out
As if God could hear only when we shout,
But I didn't get any kind of answer.

I have no desire to be young again,
Yet no desire for death, nor to be old
And sensible. For too long I have told
The young what I myself fail to avoid.

So what I want to know is just how long
Have I got – not detail, not to the day
Nor hour, just a stab at when I shall say
My last good-night, fail to rise from my chair,

Spill the last glass of wine down my shirt-front,
Or hear my daughter say, 'I'm a bit fussed ...'
Or watch the doctor mouth, 'I think I must
Tell you ...', or the nurse whisper, 'The biopsy ...'

An hour a day in the gym, on the roads,
Weights into miles, yet everything alters
And slackens, my gut sags and heart falters,
My memory sags too, and my desire.

What few words I have glitter like fools' gold.
Tell me at least how to measure the days,
How to be patient, how to learn the ways
Of assuming wisdom and serenity.

There is no comfort to be had in age,
Unless the mind slips backwards down the slope
To a child's shattered fragments, there is no hope
But the quick exit, bemused by morphine.

———

Now I am told my old friend is dying
And once more the words are taken from me.
I walk the roads around his house blindly
And cursing. He greets his death with grace.

The doctors offer him a few months more;
He turns them down, smiling; since the exit's sure,
Why search for something further? There's no cure.
He may as well die with his eyes open.

So he plans his funeral exactly,
Like a well-taught lesson: what we shall play,
What sing, what read, though with a shrug he says
He'll let the priest add some well-worn prayers.

He'll invite only friends to the funeral;
He will have none of the obsequious,
No representatives. He will free us
From the need to attend if we're busy.

After all, he'll be busy himself,
Away on a long – one might even say,
Infinitely extended – holiday;
He's busy with dying; it too takes time.

So he invites himself to stay, though only
If it really suits us. He brings old wine
And a new book, and sits down to dine
Though the cancer means that food disgusts him.

But he will die at home if possible,
With a few friends to guard him. If they're tight
That'll be their business. When the last light
Burns out he won't be around to mind them.

One shouldn't feel sad for this kind of end,
But I mourn his passing, and miss his friendship,
The funny letters on ballet and books,
And the straight talking. Amen, old friend.

Amen.

―――

To You I turn, O heavy-handed God,
To You I turn again, who eats our hearts
Before we're even old, who tears the shirts
From off our backs, to get us well-prepared

For punishment. For years I lived in peace
Without You, so why should I need You now?
Is there all that much which I still don't know.
I'm not a child who needs Your comforting.

I rage at this undesired intrusion,
This trespass of my privacy, this gross
Uncalled-for interference, this loss
Of space. You have taken me from myself.

What have I done that You should pity me?
Am I a sojourner again, an exile?
Just another name on a dusty file?
I cannot bear the thought of still more death.

The wind has tugged all day at this frail shack
On stilts above the river. One would think
Now that it's dark the wind would at last sink
A notch or two, but still it moans away

Like a mad patient. The distant surf
Mumbles disorderly music. The more
I turn the pages, the more they ignore
All sense, all purpose. I have lost my way.

There's nothing I want for, nothing I want.
I have had so much, yet I hunger.
I am blessed in love, yet live in anger.
In my strength, I rage at decrepitude.

I have learned nothing from experience;
There is no one who hears one word I say
And what I write tonight I shall destroy
Tomorrow. Only the wind has a voice.

Halfway to heaven

'Let not my slippery footsteps slide ...'

In the margins
Fence and hedgerow
Field and wild wood
Long forgotten
Soon concealed
Falls the footpath
Down the hillside
Halfway somewhere.

Nowhere going
Nothing knowing
Silence only
Almost lonely
Striding streamwards
Trudging hill-high
Downland going
Upland slowing.

Inland seagulls
Storms at seaside
Fallen willows
Streaming bridges
Winter ploughing
Frost has broken –
Hazy greening
Edges vision.

All on purpose
All designed
Man-made landscape
Nature's lordling –
Thus we journey
In our walking
Heaven's wayfare
Halfway homewards.

It is one of those days when you might almost believe in heaven:
Early spring, well before Easter, and when you look across the fields
It's as if the harrowed lands had been washed with water-colour
Or the sun had a green filter – cold still, so you half-wish for gloves
But don't really need them. Most of all, it's the birds which let you
      know
This is spring, not late winter: too busy to be alarmed, until
You are near them, and then the blackbird's shrill chink-chink-
      chink as he flees…
But this is nearly all love-song, which should be sad, though it isn't –
Wren, robin, mistle-thrush, song-thrush, bull-finch, gold-crest and
      fly-catcher,
And the wood-pigeon's noisy aerial sidestep as he dodges
Upward through the trees.

England just before spring; sojourner's home, and content to be here,
Sky still misty, not yet bleached into summer and its bluey-white,
Field-fare and red-wing with their instinct for leaving, and the breezes
Bringing a taste of salt up from the furrows and dykes of the
      marshland.

And here on the by-way a farm-hand walking back from early work
With a bag on his back, a greeting, a word about the weather,
Then resumes his trudging to the footpath bordering two counties,
Six hundred years or more in the making, often the least likely
Although one learns after a while where a wayfarer would have
      walked,
Not that streaming valley but the slight rise to the even older road
Which takes the high-way to the coastline before the harbours silted.
We shall come to heaven in time, probably down an older road
Than we remember, when there slip into our heads words from
      childhood
So often repeated we suppose we must have thought them ourselves.

Although, at times, we seem in doubt
         Which way to walk,
It's you who always chooses darkling lanes
Below the arching ancient hedgerow trees
     While I will choose the upland way
     In hope to glimpse across the bay
     Sunlight on the blue-grey seas.

     Although, at times, we seem unsure
          Which way to go,
Then each will take the other's longed-for road;
I choose what I am sure you would decide,
     And you will choose for me
     The upward climb to view the sea
     Past the point where hills divide.

     But always, love, we do not choose
          To walk apart,
For you to go alone the sheltered way,
Or me to struggle up the steeper side.
     We take the path that we
     Suppose the other wants to see:
     Love agreed and choice denied.

Three elegies

War-grave

Brown's Wood; a cemetery in northern France;
And unnumbered numbered graves. It's the scale
That's so hard to take in, the hill on hill
Of white and wooden crosses, named, unnamed.

We've often meant to stop while going south
On summer pilgrimage, but always found
The lure of sun and beaches dragged us past
The little roads which bring one to this place.

I've come at last to view a single grave:
My father's father, Private Harry Driver,
Killed in nineteen-sixteen, aged thirty-two;
Survived a fortnight only, at the front.

The regimental history merely states
Most men were lost advancing down a road;
'Took many casualties' is the phrase they used,
Though 'many murdered' might have been more truthful.

We find the section, then the row, and then
The numbered cross and grave. I check the slip
To make quite sure. It's my grandfather's grave.
Is it from this death that I began to grow?

And what's the sense of this, I ask. To come
To where the body lies (now dust of dirt
Or bones beside) a continent from home
Of someone whom his own son hardly knew?

I stand beside his grave to say a prayer
For Harry Driver, and the rest like him,
On whom the guns were trained before they moved
That morning down the deadly sunken road.

I cannot make the slightest sense of all
These deaths. If God exists, He must have shut
His eyes, or else would intervene to stop
This slaughter. But God cannot hide His eyes.

A ballad of uncles

i.m. Charles Terry Gould, d. 1941
Astley John ('Jimmy') Gould, d. 1942

Jimmy was a gunner: Lieutenant Gould,
    A vicar's son, handsome,
Tall and wavy-haired, distinguished
    In uniform.

His brother Charles – the older – an airman
    Who drove a tatty car (he tied
Its bonnet on with string), a lad
    With girls beside –

And bedside too, his sisters blushed to say.
    When wartime came, they both
Kissed the parents, their sisters too,
    And went up north –

And then went west, the pair of them, a year
    Apart. Jimmy always said
He'd live beyond the war, but Charles
    Knew he'd be dead.

He told his crew there was still a fault
    In the little plane he flew;
Three times he took it up to check,
    The fourth he flew

Into a mountain-side. And Jimmy fought
    On, riding with his troop
In search of tanks in the desert,
        To set a trap

That'd hold the rear while the rest ran from Rommel.
    He'd say, Give us a start,
We'll outrun any Eyetie, and most Germans.
        Luck fell apart

When shells fell in the trench he had chosen.
    He died of wounds next day
On a hospital ship at Tobruk
        Out in the bay.

'It's fifty years ...'

It's fifty years, almost to the actual day,
My father walked along this beach with me.
The dunes have changed, but it's the same wild sea
Where Dias Rock juts into Bushman's Bay

Like a fist. He'd come back at last, from war
Up north, and then a prison camp: a priest,
Huge and gentle, whose photograph I'd kissed
Each night for years, until I hardly saw

My father's face above the uniform. But now
I had a father in the flesh, and knew
He'd be around for years, till I too grew
As big, and strong enough to lift a boy

One-handed to the rocks above the surf,
Where broken waves ran, clash and cross, and swirled
On hidden shelves of rock, until they curled
Back fierce and upwards in a blue-green curve.

We must have fished; he would have smoked his pipe
And read; and I think I must have found a pool
Of sea-anemones, and hermit-crabs, a school
Of small translucent fish which swooped too deep

For hands to catch. I don't remember more
About that day, except the windswept walk
Along a beach, and waves. If there was talk,
It wasn't of the war, or camps, for sure.

I think of him today, a silent man
Who walks this curving beach, and sometimes smiles
To see his son try matching strides, for miles
On stubborn miles, until, one day, too soon,

The father's gone, and all my answers, too.
I walk this beach alone, and watch my stride
Get shorter, till it merges with the tide,
And wish I knew more than I find I do.

Love-song in old age

I walked outside
And saw, with surprise,
As if I had new eyes,
You in your chair, reading,
Stretched out sleekly
In the sunshine,
Young again.

And you looked up
In the hard-edged sun
And said, 'You look so young
Standing there watching me;
I was dozing
In the sunshine
Like a seal.'

To the old you
I said, 'O my dear,
I see now that you wear
Your years like finery.'
And you replied,
Smiling, that time
Beguiles us.

And then the sun
Shifted sideways slightly
And you laughed lightly,
You in your chair, reading,
And I watching,
And we were both
Ourselves again.

In the flotsam you may find –
Surprise – what still surprises:
Jewels, jetsam, detritus
Of seaweed and shell, broken,
Half-broken, whole, imperfect,
Whirl of the waves retreating
Etched on the sea-sand briefly,
Whorl of the innermost shell
As pale as the rock-pool sand,
Intricate wind and the waves
Sculpt sand-dune and (so sudden)
O what silence is falling ...

Late night: waking

Late at night I wake; I'm still downstairs;
The lights are on, the doors are open wide,
The screen is blank, the novel on my knees
Open at a page I do not think I read.

The house is silent; just a modicum
Of night-breeze flicks the curtain's lower edge
And fills the room with scent, honeysuckle
Jasmine, roses. I cannot hear my wife –

She must have gone to bed, and left me here,
And now I'm hardly fit to shift myself
From out this awkward comfy rocking chair;
My knees are older than the rest of me.

At the garden door I stand, staring out
At scented summer night. There's too much light
To see the stars, but even if I could
I do not know my way around this sky.

An owl is tracing maps below the house,
From tree to lake to copse, and back again;
Unlike this ancient exiled sojourner,
He knows precisely where his place should be.

You'd think, with so much here, with so much here,
I'd be content at last. Who'd ask for more
Than summer nights like this, in garden rooms,
And wife and children safe and sound asleep?

Suddenly I see, walking up the lawn,
My father: big, familiar as myself,
His face half-hidden in the dark, but stiff-kneed
Shamble exactly as it used to be.

I'm still asleep; this is another dream –
My father come again to visit me,
In England, as I longed for him to do.
'I saw you standing in the light,' he says,

'It's strange how much alike we are; I thought
For half a moment that it might be me
Standing in the doorway there.' It's my son,
And not my father. I'm awake. I knew.

This is the one who walks at night. 'You're late,'
I say, and he replies, 'You were asleep
So soundly in your chair, mouth open wide,
Like an old man. I bent to hear you breathe,'

As once I too would kneel beside his bed
To make quite sure he really was alive,
And say a prayer, although I knew quite well
What little chance there was of prayers being heard.

I do not tell him who I thought he was –
He'll have time enough to know, when he's old
And struggles up from his chair to look out
At summer night in an entranced garden

Where sons and fathers merge in one patterned
Circumstance of summer scent and northern light,
Of owls who pace their close dominions
To make a map of home. I live here now.

Upstairs my wife is sound asleep. My son
Stands by my side, to watch the shadowed lawn
And hedges. I am at home in England,
At home as much as I shall ever be.

Lightly my strong son hugs me his goodnight
And I reply in kind, my height to height,
To flesh my flesh, and of my father's, too.
These garden ghosts have friendly eyes.
     Goodnight.

In a rich man's garden

From this high hill one seems to see
Almost half of England: a green half,
For sure, miles of field and hedgerow,
Woods as once all England had them,
And here the Thames so sweetly flows,
Somnambulating, deeply green.

The garden preens itself, in sun up here,
In golden green, in maple red,
In yellow too – an early oak,
Laburnum, willow, broom. Festooned
With petals from an apple tree,
The lawn is like a bridal veil.

Below the dapples of the pond
The carp (or are they koi?) process
As calm and slow as cardinals,
Robed in red and gold. Watching them,
A marble naiad almost smiles,
Languidly between her cupids.

A gilded girl, naked on her perch,
Dives like a swallow down and down –
Never moves. Sky behind is all
That falls. Silver snakes entwine
(Pure illusion this) sinuous
As if the arms of Indian dancers.

And here against a hedge of fir
Posed in bronze a scene of soldiers,
Tongues stuck out, cocks and balls exposed,
Who pirouette with parachutes,
Propellers on their backs, and poise
Before they do not launch themselves:

The strangest war forever fought
With weapons not designed to kill,
And ladders not to climb, above
A sea of grass where lurk the shapes
Of sharks and other hooded things,
Like death and all his intimates.

Secluded in a corner stands
A sculpted maiden, hardly grown,
Gagged and handcuffed. Who hid her here?
Who thought to make this almost child
Almost trapped like this? Is this art
Which places monsters on a lawn?

Here there's time to stare at England,
To wonder where we went, and why.
What money made, consumed, displayed,
As if the only other way
Would be a rapt eternity
Where what we earned is what we got.

Elsewhere

We drove too hard and fast all day,
Halfway across the old country,
Then spent the night airbound,
Chairbound,
Hardly sleeping.
The first day back,
No sleep either, not dozing even –
Sundries and shopping,
Mundane and ethereal messages,
Solicitudes and solicitations –
Trappings of normal English life –
And then, at last, though late, to bed,
As good as dead, at once …

Until, in blackout dark,
I woke, not knowing:
Where I was, whose house,
Which room, who lay
Far away on the bedside.
Where the door, the light-switch?
And who was I?
No, worse than that: not who, but what,
Something massed and heavy, slumped and squat,
Like a dead bull in a slaughterhouse.

At first I thought I'd had a stroke –
I couldn't find my voice, nor any words,
And then that maybe I was really dead –
A tall man fallen from the edge of sleep
Deep into a pit.

Perhaps she heard me fall
Or sensed my far-down fear:
Turn on the light, she said;
Don't be afraid; don't mind waking me –

You merely woke from far too deep
And far too quick.
I couldn't shift you when I came to bed.
You must have gone away again,
Somewhere else inside your head.

Twenty two thousand nights
So far
And not that many more to come
I fear.
I have lived elsewhere all my life.

Not

for Dan Jacobson

Shocking, is it not, that nothing comes
Entirely for free? Take this garden,
Now, for instance, snow-bound in late winter,
Narcissi flattened, and a song-thrush
Which scrapes for snails, as if demented.
    It's not as if one noticed less.

Or take, for instance, love. Resigned, one is,
For just about the most of time, until
There hoves in view another chance. Too late,
One says, and turns away. It's not so much
The fear of consequence: desire has died.
    It's not as if one wanted less.

Not 'perhaps', this 'not'; just a blank No,
Nothing doing, and nothing done; 'niks nie',
Doubly negative, like a blind man's stare,
And born like that, of the first nothing made,
Only that which is before and after.
    It's not as if one mattered less.

And so confirmed in abnegation
One claims that gold is got by labour
Or is dross (an older cadence, that,
Although it still applies; human nature,
If it changes, does so very slowly).
    It's not as if one struggled less.

I draw my pension now, yet sit all day
And hardly turn a page; I doze, and say
That I've been thinking; I draw the curtain shut
Because the sun is bright, and back again
Because it's dark. Turn up the sound, I pray.
    It's not as if I didn't hear.

Pas de réponse

Rain on a foreign river, late rain, late –
Late in the season, old man, late at night
(Or does this count as early morning?) …

Light on the grey slate roofs, on the turrets
And crenellations of the rampart walls
Useless in a city now stretched too far …

Night-time wind, well past midnight, not yet dawn
(Why has nobody turned those lights out?)
And rain so strong it tugs the sky sideways …

Lights as bright as a prison-yard, no one
Moving down there, no one braving a move
And the rain confining my wakefulness.

Is there no one else awake in this city
In the rain, under the teeming rain,
Beyond the fierce white lights in the darkness?

A Karoo garden

for Maeder and Lesley Osler

There's a hoopoe on the lawn
searching in the morning light
to find what the night has brought.

I too have been up since dawn
having hardly slept last night
(we drank much more than I thought)

and have been searching for words,
staring out at the morning,
in hope that the haze will lift.

I'm distracted by the birds
(all repeat the tunes they sing)
and the early breezes shift

long shadows across the grass:
copper prunis, elder, pine,
willow, weeping mulberry,

and a towering cypress.
I walk out in the sunshine
to name the flowers: peri-

winkle, larkspur, columbine,
daisies in white confusion,
lilies, aloes, marigolds,

irises and trumpet-vine –
disorderly profusion
enclosed in the ample folds

of old stone-and-mortar walls.
I look from the garden's edge
to the wild Karoo outside

as it lifts to the near hills
and on to a mountain ridge
jutting gauntly the far side

of the dry levels, and then
upwards, sky-high, to the sound
of clapper larks whistling far.

As walls define this garden,
coming here again I've found
what it was I waited for.

In Cape Town again

for Neville Rubin

They're doves which wake us these days,
Urgently repetitive
And ludicrously early.
>   *To-rue-to-to-to-rue-to,*
>   *To-rue-to-to-to-rue-to ...*
Were once the secret policemen,
Savage in their sarcasm,
Ponderoso accurate:
>   *We've come to search these premises,*
>   *We've come to search these premises*
What offence do you perceive
To wake us up so early,
So ludicrously early?
>   *We have reasons to suspect,*
>   *We have reasons to suspect.*
We shall sit out in the sun,
On the far side of the house,
Drinking coffee on the patio ...
>   *We know you're hiding something,*
>   *We know you're hiding something.*
What threat are you under now
To wake so early, prisoner,
So ludicrously early
(Unimportant suspect now,
Middle-aged, respectable)?
>   *Are you thinking thoughts again?*
>   *Are you thinking thoughts again?*
Who knows what our dreams have done
To us in the dark, the deep?
Sea-weed twines around our limbs,
Drags us down, down deeper still.
>   *And we don't need a warrant,*
>   *And we don't need a warrant*

What twists there are, what false turns,
Subterfuge and misdirection,
What secrets kept, truths untold,
And lies, blurted out in fear?
>   *You will tell us in a while,*
>   *You will tell us in a while.*
All the same, let us agree:
Peace is better than nightmares.
Across the road from the old days,
We sit on a verandah,
Sipping wine (both sweet and cold),
Ludicrously early,
Throwing breadcrumbs to the doves.
>   *You will sign this statement now.*
>   *You will sign this statement now.*

A meditation

for Nadine Gordimer's 75th birthday

Action is deceit; what one needs most of all
Is to sit still, to wait and to look –
One might even want to call it *Being patient*
If one wasn't so busy with the detail:
Four figures in a landscape; three poplars
Positioned in a quarry; two pied crows;
And Mohammed Ismael's general store
On a roadside in the middle of nowhere.

That's what novelists do. As Auden said,
Art makes nothing happen, so to be old
Becomes an advantage. One sees further;
Oh, the broad brushstroke, the sweep – well, call it
'History' if you really must, but it's more …
What makes this entirely this, and not that:
And one notes it down, unreservedly,
Telling lies to make imaginary truth.

And the people too, poor forked beings,
Whom one thinks one sees so clearly, until
They do something odd, as in eating apples,
And one's surprised, even though one made them.
What they should see is what one lets them see,
But then they see much further than one thought
And they add a sentence that's not one's own –
Almost, sometimes, at dictation speed.

And the desire for change? One has that too,
Though to confuse what is with what should be
Is dangerous romance, enemy of art,
And time will sort that out, quickly – or so

One has to hope, or else there's not much point
In all this striving, hours, and days, and months
And then years, and tens of years, piled up high
Like a builder's yard, all the bits and pieces
Which may one day make – who knows? – a palace.

My hands ache sometimes and, when I look up
From the keyboard, even the wall is blurred.

Elegy for Joseph Brodsky

You can pick up the pieces, but not quickly: glitter, glitz even,
Slivers of ice on black water, like the old city, like heaven.
For God's sake, this is America. I'm nameless. There are Brodskys
In every state, in every phonebook, crowds of us under broad skies
With urban horizons, singular people, one of everyone,
Noisy, guttural, given to languages, others and our own.
We'd known nightguards, and dayguards, and stupid judges,
   the crumpled grass
Of the central compound, then caught exile like a sudden illness.

There's much you can change, and more that you can't;
   in the end what matters –
Words on the page, shards of laughter, what the pine-tree mutters
And the music repeats – are the old uncertainties
   (we'll never bloody know
Whatever the footnotes pretend) until suddenly soon means now
And you're dead. Like that. Emptied. Stubbed out. Undone.
      And that day I missed
The obits, and later read, 'May I add something?' And then realised.
It's not as if a species had died, or the people, but we'll miss
You in particular, Joseph Brodsky, once more at the wrong address.

Skylark

The last lark in England
Is calling me to look away
From where its eggs must lie
Stranded in this 'set-aside':
Hedgeless pasture ploughed three years ago
Rank with thistles now,
Ragwort, mallow, speedwell,
Ox-eyed daisies (as if someone put them there) –
The oddest dereliction.

Only once I've come across a nest
And that was when I didn't try;
I veered from where the footpath curved,
And there they were:
Three tiny eggs in camouflage,
Greyish green, and marked in olive-brown,
Almost as if they'd been scribbled on,
Held in less than half a hand
Of undistinguished earth.

I know how little point there is
To search for what comes unannounced
But still I shift my track again
In hope, but hardly expectation,
Though once I did, and may do once again.
The lark repeats its call
Look up, look up, look up –
And I look down
To where one step would end this song.

A little late song

The wind clowns about
As a dog jumps to catch a kite
Howling down on him
On the Clifton Downs.
Over there's my wife, reading in the cold,
A hood over her head,
And the newspapers trying to escape.
There's my tall daughter, smiling
As her husband hugs her.
Here am I, walking towards them,
Over the short April grass,
On a Sunday, in the new century.

Karoo concert

for Camilla Driver

In the magical dusk
On a table-top koppie, sacred with engraving,
In the far hills above the river,
Seated at the sounding stones,
My cousin (removed by a generation)
A musician (violinist mainly)
Strikes three notes and pronounces:
'A perfect fourth'.
She turns herself sideways and strikes again,
To find the complicated natural seventh,
Which predates the approximation of the piano
And reverberates now in the almost darkness.

Around us the various ghosts listen,
Some entranced, some quizzical
At this knowledgeable intrusion.
One old man mutters to another:
'She's of marriageable age
And has useful skills
Evident in this music.'

Sunbird

Cape sugarbird,
Malachite sunbird,
And drab something,
Probably female.

Sunbrown face,
Grey-white panache, brushed back,
Plumage grey and black,
Gold at neck and wrist.

Glasses too big for her,
Legs as skinny
As a sandpiper's –
But longer.

Migrates when required
But would rather not;
Prefers deep woodland,
Gardens and small houses.

Fierce when cornered,
Though mainly peaceable;
Call often imitates
Other species.

Uxorious, absent-minded,
Seldom solitary;
Protects her young,
Mates for life.

Creation

Who made man? God made man, in His Image.
Who made razor-wire? Man made razor-wire,
In rage.
Which then stretches higher,
God or razor-wire?
Turn the page.

BY THE SAME AUTHOR

Novels:
Elegy for a Revolutionary
Send War In Our Time, O Lord
Death of Fathers
A Messiah of the Last Days
Shades of Darkness
Biography:
Patrick Duncan, South African and Pan-African
Poetry:
Occasional Light (with Jack Cope)
I Live Here Now
Hong Kong Portraits
In the Water-Margins
Holiday Haiku
Requiem

ACKNOWLEDGEMENTS

Most of these poems have been published before in various magazines and periodicals, including *Contrast, The New African, New Classic, New Contrast, The London Magazine, The New Review, The Times Literary Supplement, Workshop, Proof, South African Outlook, Solstice, Tracks, New Coin, Carapace,* the *South China Morning Post* and *Oxford Today.* Some of the poems have appeared in anthologies, including *London Magazine Poems 1961–66* (selected by Hugo Williams, Alan Ross, 1966), the *Penguin Book of South African Verse* (ed. Cope and Krige, 1968), *Seven South African Poets* (ed. Cosmo Pieterse, Heinemann, 1971), *New Poetry 3* (ed. Alan Brownjohn and Maureen Duffy, Arts Council, 1977), *A Century of South African Poetry* (ed. Michael Chapman, Ad. Donker, 1981), *Momentum* (ed. M J Daymond, J U Jacobs, Margaret Lenta, University of Natal, 1984), *Poetry Works* (ed. Robin Malan, David Philip, 1995), *The Heart In Exile* (ed. Leon de Kock and Ian Tromp, Penguin, 1996), *Soundings* (ed. Douglas Reid Skinner, Carrefour Press, 1996) and *Worldscapes* (ed. Robin Malan, Oxford, 1997). Some of the early poems appeared under the title, 'Occasional Light', in a book shared with Jack Cope in the Mantis Poets series (David Philip, 1979), and others in *I Live Here Now* (Paperback Poets 9, Lincolnshire and Humberside Arts, 1979). The 'Hong Kong Portraits' were first broadcast by RTHK (Hong Kong) and were then published by the Perpetua Press in 1986. *In The Water-Margins,* which included *The Journey Back,* was published by Snailpress in association with Crane River Press in 1994. *Holiday Haiku* was published as a pamphlet by Snailpress in 1997, and *Requiem* by the Belgrave Press in 1998. 'What The Stones Said to Michael Rostrow' is the postscript to a story, 'False, Impossible Shore' in *Penguin Modern Stories* 8, and 'A Meditation' first appeared in *A Writing Life, Celebrating Nadine Gordimer* (ed. Andries Walter Oliphant, Penguin 1998).

BIOGRAPHICAL NOTE

Born in Cape Town in 1939, CJ (Jonty) Driver spent the years of the Second World War in Kroonstad with his mother and younger brother; his maternal grandfather was the Anglican rector there. His father fought through North Africa, then was captured at Tobruk and spent the rest of the war as a prisoner in Italy and Germany. When he came back, the family moved to Grahamstown in the Eastern Cape, where his father was chaplain of St Andrews College, to which Jonty Driver went as a pupil in due course.

After most of a year teaching in what was then Rhodesia, and five years at the University of Cape Town, he was elected President of the National Union of South African Students in 1963 and again in 1964. In August and September 1964, he was locked up by the police in solitary confinement, ostensibly on suspicion of his involvement in the African Resistance Movement, and immediately afterwards left for England.

After a year's teaching, he went to Trinity College, Oxford, to read for an M.Phil, and afterwards returned to teaching, at Sevenoaks School and then Matthew Humberstone Comprehensive School. While he was at Oxford, the South African authorities refused to renew his passport and he became stateless for several years, eventually becoming a British citizen. For more than twenty years he was prohibited from returning to South Africa.

For twenty-three years he was a headmaster (Principal, Island School, Hong Kong, 1978–83; Headmaster, Berkhamsted School, 1983–9; Master, Wellington College, 1989–2000). He is now a full-time writer, though he continues his involvement in education, particularly as a governor of various schools, including Millfield, Benenden and Milton Abbey. He has been a Trustee of the Beit Trust since 2000. He is married with three adult children, and he and his wife live in East Sussex.